TROUBLEMAKERS
AMERICAN

Jefferson Davis: Confederate President

T★AMERICAN★S TROUBLEMAKERS

JEFFERSON DAVIS:
Confederate President

Robert R. Potter

With an Introduction by James P. Shenton

RSVP
RAINTREE
STECK-VAUGHN
P U B L I S H E R S
The Steck-Vaughn Company

Austin, Texas

CONSULTANTS
Ola Mae Dana
American History Teacher
Long Beach Middle School
Long Beach, Mississippi

James P. Shenton
Professor of History
Columbia University
New York, New York

MANAGING EDITOR
Richard Gallin

PROJECT MANAGER
Cynthia Ellis

PHOTO EDITOR
Margie Foster

A Gallin House Press Book

Library of Congress Cataloging-in-Publication Data
Potter, Robert R. (Robert Russell)
    Jefferson Davis: Confederate president / written by Robert R. Potter.
        p.   cm. — (American Troublemakers)
    "A Gallin House Press Book."
    Includes bibliographical references and index.
    Summary: A biography of the soldier and statesman who became the president of the Confederacy during the Civil War.
    ISBN 0-8114-2330-1
    1. Davis, Jefferson, 1808-1889 — Juvenile literature.   2. Presidents — Confederate States of America — Biography — Juvenile literature.   3. Statesmen —United States — Biography — Juvenile literature.   [1. Davis, Jefferson, 1808-1889.   2. Presidents — Confederate States of America.] I.Title.   II. Series.
    E467.1.D26P58   1994
    973.7'13'092—dc20
    [B]   92-16914
                                                                  CIP
                                                                  AC

Printed and bound in the United States.
1 2 3 4 5 6 7 8 9 LB 98 97 96 95 94 93

CONTENTS

Maps

Jefferson Davis

INTRODUCTION

by James P. Shenton

Biography is the history of the individual lives of men and women. In all lives, there is a sequence that begins with birth, evolves into the development of character in childhood and adolescence, is followed by the emergence of maturity in adulthood, and finally concludes with death. All lives follow this pattern, although with each emerge the differences that make each life unique. These distinctive characteristics are usually determined by the particular area in which a person has been most active. An artist draws his or her specific identity from the area of the arts in which he or she has been most active. So the writer becomes an author; the musician, a performer or composer; the politician, a senator, governor, president, or statesperson. The intellectual discipline to which one is attached identifies the scientist, historian, economist, literary critic, or political scientist, among many. Some aspects of human behavior are identified as heroic, cowardly, corrupt, or just ordinary. The task of the biographer is to explain why a particular life is worth remembering. And if the effort is successful, the reader draws from it insights into a vast range of behavior patterns. In a sense, biography provides lessons from life.

Some lives become important because of the position a person holds. Typical would be that of a U.S. President in which a biographer compares the various incumbents to determine their comparative importance. Without question, Abraham Lincoln was a profoundly significant President, much more so than Warren G. Harding whose administration was swamped by corruption. Others achieve importance because of their role in a particular area. So Emily Dickinson and Carl Sandburg are recognized as important poets and Albert Einstein as a great scientist.

Implicit in the choice of biographical subjects is the idea that each somehow affected history. Their lives explain something about the world in which they lived, even as they affect our lives and that of generations to come. But there is another consideration: Some lives are more interesting than those of others. Within each life is a great story that illuminates human behavior.

Then there are those people who are troublemakers, people whom we cannot ignore. They are the people who both upset and fascinate us. Their singular quality is that they are uniquely different. Troublemakers are irritating, perhaps frightening, frustrating, and disturbing, but never dull. They march to their own drummer, and they are original.

Forty-two men have been President of the United States. Only one man was president of the Confederate States of America. He was Jefferson Davis, born in Kentucky only a short distance from the birthplace of his archfoe Abraham Lincoln. Unlike Lincoln, whose reputation shimmers in the light of the Northern victory, Davis's reputation has been shadowed by the fact that he led the Confederacy into total war and defeat. He had the further misfortune of being decreed a traitor. Nonetheless, this dour man gave the Confederacy a leadership that brought it to the brink of victory.

Before the Civil War, Jefferson Davis seemed an ordinary politician. He served both as U.S. senator from Mississippi and U.S. secretary of war efficiently and effectively. Politically committed to states' rights, Davis gave his first loyalty to the state rather than to the federal government. As the crisis of the Union deepened during the 1850s, he strongly defended Southern interests without taking a leading position in the disruption of the Union. Once secession came, he never looked backward. As the Confederacy took shape, its founders concluded that he was the logical first president of the new country. His Mexican War experience reenforced his belief that he knew how to guide a country at war. Forceful, arrogantly self-assured, and determined, Jefferson Davis assumed a nearly dictatorial leadership. It often seemed that his willpower alone would overcome the material deficiencies that blocked a Southern victory. Even as doom encroached upon the Confederacy, he pursued tenaciously Southern independence. It was as if he believed his willpower and the Confederacy were one.

With the fall of Richmond in April 1865, Jefferson Davis fled south to continue a hopeless war. Captured and imprisoned, he never doubted the correctness of the course he had followed. When he died twenty-four years after Appomattox, he remained a troublesome reminder to the North that the conquered South had never surrendered its spirit.

CHAPTER ONE

Two Births in Kentucky

In mid-1808 and early 1809, two famous men were born in the state of Kentucky, about a hundred miles apart. Both were born in log cabins. Both were born into hardworking pioneer families. Both would leave Kentucky as children, one for the North, the other for the South.

Fifty-two years later, the two men would again be about a hundred miles apart. In Washington, D.C., Abraham Lincoln would be President of the United States. In the spring of 1861, Lincoln could look out the White House windows and see the Confederate flag flying on Munson's Hill, across the Potomac River in the state of Virginia. Beyond Munson's Hill, beyond many more hills and across several rivers, lay Richmond, Virginia, the capital of the Confederacy. There in Richmond, in a building also called the White House, sat Jefferson Davis, president of the Confederate States of America. The Civil War had started, but the bullets had hardly begun to fly. Neither president thought that the war would take four more years and the lives of about 625,000 American men and boys.

This book is the true story of the firstborn of these two principled but different men, Jefferson Davis.

Jefferson Davis was born on June 3, 1808, in what is now Todd County, Kentucky. In this instance, perhaps only one of the two words *log cabin* is strictly correct. True, the building was built of logs, from trees cut down by pioneer Samuel Davis as he cleared land on what was to be his family's new and better farm. But by the time little Jeff was born,

Building a log house.

9

the cabin had four rooms. It also had what was rare in Todd County—windows made of real glass. If it was a log cabin, it was also something of a settler's showplace.

Jefferson's mother, Jane Davis, had already given birth to nine children in twenty-three years. She was forty-six. Samuel Davis was just over fifty. The parents named the new baby Jefferson for one of their heroes, Thomas Jefferson, third President of the United States. The child's middle name, Finis, is Latin for "the end." At their ages, Jane and Samuel Davis probably expected that their tenth baby would be their last.

When Jefferson was born, the United States of America was a far different country from what it is today. There were only seventeen states. Florida belonged to Spain. The whole Southwest — from Texas to the coast of California—was part of the Viceroyalty of Mexico, ruled by Spain. Railroads were as yet fantasies of the future. So were such simple inventions as the telegraph and the sewing machine. Most Americans were farmers who measured their wealth in land, horses, oxen, and—in the South—slaves.

Yet the United States was also a rapidly expanding nation. Wherever a person lived, travelers were always coming back from the West with tales of rich soil and richer opportunities. The West was a dream that a person could make come true—simply by pulling up stakes, loading everything the family owned into wagons and onto horses, and setting forth as a pioneer.

Such a person was Jefferson Davis's father. Samuel Emory Davis was a native of Georgia. After four years of service in the Revolutionary War, he had been given government land near Augusta to start a farm. There his gritty determination and hard work had paid off. He had done well. As the unusual farmer who could read and write like a schoolteacher, he had served as county clerk and taken on other important jobs. But like many people at the time, he had itchy feet and higher hopes. Fifteen years before Jefferson's birth, he had moved his family, his livestock, and his few slaves up through Tennessee and into Kentucky. There he had worked side by side with his slaves, dawn to dusk, in fields of tobacco. On the side, he raised fine horses and even opened his crowded house to strangers as a wayside inn.

But the West still called him. When little Jeff was two, Samuel made plans to move again. This time he would go not northwest but southwest, across the Mississippi River into lower Louisiana Territory. The trip took weeks and weeks. At the end of the road, Samuel knew, would be good soil and a new crop—cotton. This, he believed, was the road to riches. Cotton was now the crop that could make a man wealthy in only a few years. "King Cotton," it was called. King Cotton was summoning thousands of loyal subjects into the region near the lower Mississippi River, where the crop grew well.

In lower Louisiana Territory, Samuel Davis found just the land he wanted. But he also found something he did not want at all. In the summer, the area was horribly hot and very humid. The region produced mosquitoes as easily as it did cotton. The mosquitoes themselves were a never-ending nuisance, not a real danger. What was dangerous was the disease that the mosquitoes carried—malaria. Malarial fever could usually be controlled with quinine and other drugs, but it could also lead to death.

Slave workers not only planted and harvested cotton, they also pressed it into bales for shipment to factories.

Soon Samuel Davis got the urge to move again. As Jefferson later put it, his father wanted "higher and healthier" land. He found it in the very southwest corner of Mississippi Territory, near the small village of Woodville. Land was cleared, plowed, and planted to cotton. Before long, Samuel Davis found time to build a house that made the old Kentucky home look like a shack. The new frame house had cypress siding, porches, and dormer windows. Upstairs were two large bedrooms, one for the boys, the other for the girls. Downstairs were a kitchen, a large central hall, a master bedroom—even a separate room for eating!

Samuel and Jane Davis had been right about two things. Mississippi cotton did provide a better life than Kentucky tobacco. And their youngest son's middle name, Finis, did seem to have been well chosen. Jane Davis had no more children. A loving and level-headed woman, Jane Davis now had some time for her other interests. Her favorite hobby was growing flowers. She especially liked roses. In a few years, the rosebushes around the house filled the air with sweetness. Jane loved to name the different kinds of roses as she showed them to guests. At the time it was part of the Southern way of life to give names to houses. In this case the choice was a natural one—Rosemont.

At Rosemont, Jefferson Davis was to say many years later, "my memories begin." He remembered his father, a stern man who did not talk or smile easily, toiling day after day in the cotton fields with ten or twelve slaves. He remembered his mother and the roses. He remembered playing with the dogs and climbing the tall poplar trees around the house.

The Woodville school was a log cabin. It was reached by a narrow road through the woods. Luckily first-grader Jeff had his sister Mary Ellen for company. As children sometimes do, they invented a kind of bogeyman to watch for in fear. In this case, however, the bogeyman was not wholly made up. A local drunk earned his living by repairing chairs, which he often carried around the countryside on his head. The drunk hated children and would try to scare them as he stumbled along. One morning as they made their way to school, Jeff and Mary Ellen were seized with sudden fright. There in front of them, over some bushes and around a curve, were the moving chair legs of the bogeyman.

12

Mary Ellen's every nerve seemed to scream run and hide. But not Jeff. "We will not run," he stated. The two children held hands and waited. The chair legs turned out to be the antlers of a huge deer. The buck looked them over with little interest and walked off into the woods. Even at an early age, Jefferson Davis was not one to give ground or run away from danger.

Little Jeff—he was really called that—seemed to have been born under a lucky star. He had a quick mind and an active body. His light-brown hair, deep-set gray-blue eyes, high cheekbones, and strong chin made him very good-looking. As the youngest child in the family, he was adored by his mother and older sisters. If Samuel Davis did not show his feelings as openly, that was just not his nature. The serious Mr. Davis loved his last son with a silent passion.

Samuel Davis's main concern was for Jeff's education. He knew that the education offered inside the local log cabin was just as crude as the building itself. When Jeff was eight, his father had had enough of the Woodville school. Back in Kentucky, Samuel thought, was just the right school for this bright child who needed a good start for a chance in life.

One day Samuel Davis announced to the family that Jeff would be going to the College of St. Thomas Aquinas, near Springfield, Kentucky. (In those days, any kind of school could be called a college.) His wife Jane was shocked. Why, her "baby" was too little to go away to school! And a Catholic school at that! (The Davises were Baptists.) And finally, St. Thomas's was hundreds of miles away! How did her husband suppose that an eight-year-old was supposed to get there?

But Samuel Davis had made up his mind. His only problem was Jane's last objection—the trip itself. Then he learned that a friend of his, Thomas Hinds, was soon to leave for Kentucky with his family. Yes, the Hindses would be glad to take Jeff along. He would be good company for young Howell Hinds, a boy about Jeff's age. The two boys could ride ponies and easily keep up with the group. Without telling his wife Jane, Samuel secretly sent Jeff off to join the Hindses as they prepared to leave.

The trip was the first thrilling experience of Jefferson Davis's life. It was fun when they stopped at dusk to sleep beside the

13

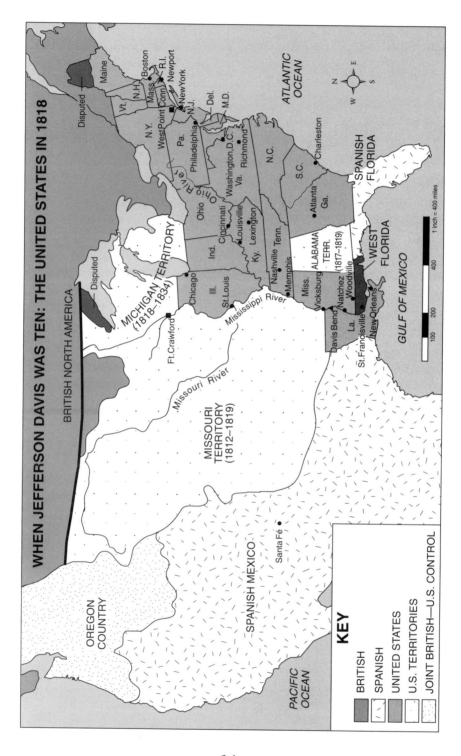

WHEN JEFFERSON DAVIS WAS TEN: THE UNITED STATES IN 1818

BRITISH NORTH AMERICA

Disputed

Disputed

MICHIGAN TERRITORY
(1818–1834)

Ft. Crawford

Chicago

Ill.

St. Louis

Ind.

Missouri River

Mississippi River

MISSOURI TERRITORY
(1812–1819)

OREGON COUNTRY

SPANISH MEXICO

Santa Fé

PACIFIC OCEAN

Maine

Vt.

N.H.

Boston
Mass.
R.I.
Newport
Conn.
New York
N.J.

N.Y.

West Point

Pa.

Philadelphia

Del.

M.D.

Washington, D.C.
Va.
Richmond

Ohio River

Ohio

Cincinnati

Louisville

Lexington

Ky.

Nashville Tenn.

Memphis

Miss.

Vicksburg
Natchez
Davis Bend
Woodville
La.
St. Francisville
New Orleans

ALABAMA TERR.
(1817–1819)

WEST FLORIDA

N.C.

S.C.

Charleston

Atlanta
Ga.

SPANISH FLORIDA

ATLANTIC OCEAN

GULF OF MEXICO

N
W   E
S

1 inch = 400 miles

100   200   400

KEY

BRITISH

SPANISH

UNITED STATES

U.S. TERRITORIES

JOINT BRITISH—U.S. CONTROL

road, making camp with the help of a trusted slave. It was even more fun when they stopped at some unknown inn for the night. The high point of the trip was a visit to Andrew Jackson near Nashville, Tennessee. Thomas Hinds had served under the hero Andrew Jackson in the War of 1812. The two men knew each other well. What started as a short visit turned out to last more than a week. When Jackson was elected president in 1828, Jefferson Davis would look back with pleasure on the days spent at his famous estate, the Hermitage.

Jeff arrived at St. Thomas College to find himself the youngest and smallest student. He soon discovered that he was the only Protestant as well. Because of these differences, one of the Catholic priests, Father William Tuite, placed a cot in his room and let Jeff live with him. But probably, Jeff needed no special protection. He got along well with his schoolmates. The young Baptist's progress, especially in Latin and Greek, pleased the priests. The Catholic school ran a farm, and probably Jeff never thought twice when he saw slaves working the fields. He had grown up with slavery; it was part of his world.

After two years, it was Jane Davis's turn to put her foot down. Her boy had been away long enough, she told her husband. Besides, now, in fact, there was finally a way for him to get home. Year by year, the steamboat runs from New Orleans had gone farther and farther up the Mississippi and Ohio rivers. By 1817, a steamboat actually managed to reach Cincinnati, Ohio. Now the steamboat line went all the way to Louisville, Kentucky. Yes, Jeff *must* come home!

For a boy Jeff's age, the steamboat trip back home must have been just as thrilling as the overland trip with the Hindses. With paddles splashing in the early summer sun, the boat made good time on the downriver trip. The steam whistle sounded as the boat approached each landing to take on or drop off freight and passengers. With the green hills of Kentucky on the left, the whispering fields and forests of Indiana and Illinois passed by on the right. Then the clear Ohio River ran into the muddy Mississippi. Past Memphis, in Tennessee, past Vicksburg and Natchez in Mississippi, the widest of all rivers snaked its way south. Between distant banks of dusty Southern green, the mighty Mississippi bent left, right, left, right, left . . . Finally the steamboat pulled up at the tiny Woodville landing. Jeff's brother Isaac was there waiting, hoping that this was the right boat. Isaac was amazed at how much Jeff had grown in two years.

As the two brothers walked home, they thought up a trick to fool their mother. Would she really be able to recognize Jeff? Nearing Rosemont, Isaac hung back. Jeff marched on alone, pretending to be the stranger he almost was. He found his mother sitting on the porch. Ma'am, had she seen any stray horses around here lately? Smiling and running forward, Jane Davis said that the only "stray" around was her long-gone son Jeff. They hugged each other. Tears poured out of joyful eyes.

The hugging and tears started again when Samuel Davis was called in from the fields. Jeff was surprised. It was more feeling than Samuel Davis had ever before allowed himself to show, or ever would again.

Jefferson Finis Davis was back at home.

CHAPTER TWO

Gifted Student and Wayward Cadet

In 1817, while Jefferson Davis was away in Kentucky at school, Mississippi was admitted to the Union as the twentieth state. In many ways, of course, Mississippi was still a raw frontier society. Fights were common. Liquor flowed freely. Men fought duels to protect their "honor"—or that of their wives.

The South of that time was also a class society. At the top came what was called the planter class. Rich plantation owners had thousands of acres and hundreds of slaves. About half of the enslaved African Americans were the property of this small group of plantation owners. Some of the planters lived in huge mansions that were maintained by black servants. Their wives dressed in lace and prided themselves on doing no work at all. Actually, most planters' wives supervised life in the mansion and kept a watch on the management of the slave cabins. They also often had to manage daily medical treatment on the plantation. To escape mosquitoes and malaria, the planters often spent the summer months in safer spots. Charleston, South Carolina, and Newport, Rhode Island, were popular.

Below the planters came the professional class—lawyers, doctors, and other experts. Well-to-do merchants were also a part of this group.

Below these came the largest group—a middle class of farmers. Some were like Samuel Davis, men who owned a few slaves and worked with them in the fields. Others worked the fields with family members and perhaps some hired help. Some of these small-farm owners were prosperous; others struggled to get by.

Then came the "poor whites" who, of course, farmed their land without slaves. Below these was a class of "pine-woods squatters," families who sweat, shivered, and nearly starved in cabins with dirt floors. They scratched the poor soil and hunted in the woods for their food. More than a few became outlaws.

In an entirely separate group were several million enslaved African Americans. A few lived fairly well, most others horribly. Life under slavery varied from place to place. About half of all enslaved black people worked on plantations as field hands, household servants, and craftspeople. The use of the whip as punishment was common. Families could be divided and individual members sold to different new owners. Over the years some African Americans were able to buy their freedom or were freed by their owners. Most free black people became farmers or worked as hired laborers or skilled craftspeople, such as blacksmiths and carpenters. Even these people did not have all the rights that white people had. Whether enslaved or free, these Americans were given the feeling that their race and African origin made them a separate and inferior people.

But now Mississippi was the twentieth state! Its proud, independent citizens held their heads up even higher. Very proud, indeed, was the family of Samuel and Jane Davis. The oldest son in the family, Joseph Davis, had written the constitution of the new state. This was a great honor.

In his own way, Joseph Davis was just as remarkable a person as his brother Jefferson. Joseph had already left home when little Jeff was born. He studied law in Kentucky. Then, like the rest of the family, he moved to Mississippi. He opened a law office in Natchez. Soon he began to buy and sell land. King Cotton forced the price of land up, up, and up. Before long, Joseph had the money to join the planter class himself. He bought thousands of acres in a big westward bend in the Mississippi River north of Natchez. Eventually he would have three hundred slaves and a yearly fortune in cotton.

But Joseph was more than a successful lawyer and planter. He was also a scholar. At one time, he had the largest private library in Mississippi. He not only had "friends in high places," but those same people looked up to him. His knowledge of history and government made him just the person to write the state constitution. Joseph also seemed to have been born an aristocrat. His ramrod-straight body moved with grace. He spoke in a polite, pleasant way that made others listen.

If there was one thing missing in the life of Joseph Davis, it

This photograph of Joseph Davis's Greek-style library and his slaves was taken in the 1860s.

was that he had no sons. All the children born to his wife were girls. This is certainly one reason that, over the years, he became like a father to little Jeff. The father-son relationship seemed a natural one, for Joseph was twenty-three years older.

In 1818, of course, ten-year-old Jeff didn't care much about his brother's huge library or the new state constitution. Jeff was about to start his teenage years. He cared about what most Southern boys cared about—guns and horses. He became a crack shot. He enjoyed hunting, alone or with friends. Samuel Davis had always kept good horses. Now Jeff stepped up from pony to horse. He was soon riding like an expert. His "seat" on a horse was erect, graceful, and commanding, elegant as a knight. To the end of his days, people would comment on the way man and horse seemed to move with one fluid motion.

Fortunately for Jeff, he didn't have to go back to the crude log schoolhouse. Soon after his return from Kentucky, a new private school opened in Woodville. Jeff attended the Wilkinson County Academy for four years. It was an excellent school, within walking distance of home. On vacations he liked to ride twenty miles across the Louisiana line to visit his sister Anna and her family. Joseph's plantation at Davis Bend was a 115-mile steamboat ride up the Mississippi.

Jefferson Davis was later to say that he learned more at the Wilkinson Academy than at any other school in his life. But not all of his memories were happy ones. At least one teacher used the old log-cabin teaching method—memorize or be whipped. One day the teacher assigned a long passage to learn by heart. Even though he had an excellent memory, little Jeff thought it was just too much. Impossible, he told the teacher. His protests bounced off deaf ears. The next day Jeff came to class unprepared. The teacher threatened the whip. Jeff simply gathered up his books and left the room. He walked home. Back at Rosemont, he told his father that he never wanted to return.

Samuel Davis could have done a number of things. He could have whipped Jeff himself. Or he could have taken Jeff's side and gone to argue with the teacher. What he actually did was this: He told Jeff that you have a choice in life, "whether you will work with head or hands." That was certain. So was the fact that Jeff couldn't hang around the house doing nothing. He handed Jeff a bag and told him to follow him into the fields. There Jeff picked cotton with his father and the slaves until dusk. The work was hot, boring, and backbreaking. At the end of the second day, Jeff told his father that, well, perhaps, school wasn't so bad after all.

By 1823, Jeff had learned all he could at the Wilkinson Academy. Samuel Davis already had other plans for his youngest son. Jeff was sent off to Transylvania University in Lexington, Kentucky. At the time, Transylvania was considered the Harvard of the South. It had the largest student body of any college in the United States. It also had fine teachers. Jeff's idea was to finish college and then go on to study law at the University of Virginia. He wanted to be a lawyer like his brother Joseph.

When the fall term started, Jeff found himself so well prepared that he was allowed to enter the junior class. Even though only fifteen, he seems to have been a model student. He got good grades and made friends easily. It was at Transylvania that Jeff learned the art of public speaking. Everyone in the junior class had to make ten speeches during the year. Jeff's sincere, musical voice pleased his teachers and fellow students alike. In the spring, at graduation time, the college put on a performance for the Lexington community. Jeff was chosen as a speaker. He titled his address "Friendship." The local paper reported that "Davis on Friendship made friends of his hearers." It was a good year for Jefferson Davis.

The bad news that year came by mail. Some time before, Samuel Davis had signed a form that guaranteed a loan made to a son-in-law. The son-in-law now found it impossible to pay back the money. Samuel Davis did not have the large sum either. He was threatened with the loss of Rosemont and his cotton lands. Where could he get some money? There had always been stories about some old family money that should have gone to Samuel. A desperate man, Samuel Davis traveled to Philadelphia, Pennsylvania, to see if the money was really his.

While at Transylvania, Jeff received a sad letter from Philadelphia. His father's trip had been useless. "If I had applied some thirty years ago," Samuel wrote, "I might now have been immensely rich but I fear all is lost here by the lapse of time." The sorrowful letter went on and on. It was almost like a last will and testament. Jeff would be left James Pemberton, the slave who served as Samuel's personal servant. Samuel asked Jeff to "use every possible means to acquire useful knowledge as knowledge is power the want of which has brought mischiefs and misery on your father in old age."

The serious man who had struggled almost fifty years for his family was now broken in spirit. But all was not lost—yet. Joseph saved the situation by buying Rosemont himself. Samuel returned there and planted cotton early in 1824. Then, for some reason, he had a violent quarrel with the son who was still helping him farm. Samuel took his slaves and started for Davis Bend. He arrived at Joseph's plantation broken in body as well. He died of malaria on July 4, 1824.

This was not all the bad news Jeff had to bear. Unknown to

21

The United States Military Academy at West Point in 1826.
Jefferson Davis attended West Point from 1824 to 1828.

Jeff, Joseph had used his "friends in high places" to apply for Jeff's admission to the United States Military Academy at West Point, New York. Jeff had been accepted. All he had to do was say yes.

Jefferson had little interest in West Point or a military career. He knew that at West Point he would be a freshman in 1824, not a senior. But he also knew that West Point was free. Going there would relieve Joseph of the costs of Transylvania. Finally the brothers arrived at a bargain that neither liked. Jefferson would try West Point for a year. If he still had no interest in a military life, he could return to Transylvania and a career in law.

West Point was—and is—located high above the Hudson River, about fifty miles north of New York City. In 1824, Jeff's first look at the plain gray buildings must have filled him with unknown dread. He soon learned that the cadets lived three to a room. Only eleven feet square, the rooms were more like cells. The furniture consisted of three chairs, a table, and three mattresses on the cold stone floor. The Hudson River served as West Point's bathtub. Hundreds of rules and regulations controlled the cadets' every move. The studies stressed math and engineering, neither of them Jeff's favorite subject.

Jefferson Davis had always been a model student—but no longer. He did just enough to get by. Perhaps this should not seem surprising. He had not chosen West Point in the first place. He was there to please his brother Joseph. And no longer did he go to sleep thinking of his father toiling in the cotton fields to pay the bills. So what if he didn't shine in class. So what if he got demerit after demerit for things like spitting on the floor, having a messy room, visiting during study time, absence from class, missing chapel, not marching from the mess hall, firing a gun out his window. . . . He knew just how many demerits meant being expelled, and he stayed safely within the limit.

It didn't take Jeff long to prove that he could be something of a troublemaker. By July 1825 he had gone over the edge of safety. In the summer the cadets were supposed to experience army life by living in tents. One night it rained. The tents leaked; no one could sleep. An order finally came to leave the tents, but Cadet Davis never heard it. He and some friends had decided to do the absolutely forbidden thing—pay a visit to Benny Havens.

Benny Havens had brought ruin to many a West Pointer. He ran a tavern on the banks of the Hudson, about two miles away. He offered fine food and spirits to any cadet who dared take the chance.

In the middle of that rainy night, who should walk into Benny Havens's tavern but one Captain Ethan H. Hitchcock. This was the officer whose job it was to be always on the prowl for wayward cadets. Jeff and his four friends were arrested. The next day they were thrown into the guardhouse. Their military trial, or court-martial, began the day following.

Cadet Davis served as his own lawyer. The rain, he said, had driven them from their tents. They had wandered around and finally "wandered too far." The Havens building was open and offered shelter. Moreover, Captain Hitchcock had not actually seen him drinking. (Hitchcock had testified only that Davis seemed a little drunk.) And even if he had been drinking, it would have been porter, a drink like beer. The regulation about drinking mentioned "wine or spiritous liquors." Davis argued that "spiritous liquors" meant only hard liquor, not porter.

The officers of the court were not about to believe this story. They found Davis and the others guilty. All five were ordered expelled from West Point.

As it turned out, however, only three of the five cadets were really forced to leave. Jeff spent the month of August under arrest. Then he learned that the court had recommended pardon for him and one other. By special order of the War Department in Washington, the two were readmitted.

Had Cadet Davis learned his lesson? Hardly. The next summer he and a friend again found their way into Benny Havens's tavern. Someone came in to say that Hitchcock or another officer was coming. The two drinkers ran from the tavern in panic. Wanting to avoid Hitchcock, they kept off the road that led up to the Point. Instead, they scrambled along a cliff above the Hudson River. The drink must have affected Jeff's footing, for suddenly he slipped. He plunged more than fifty feet down the cliff, trying to stop himself by reaching for trees and rocks. Then silence.

"Jeff, are you dead?" came a voice from above.

All Jeff could do was raise a bloody hand. If he could have spoken, he might have answered the question yes. He was badly hurt. His head and body injuries kept him in the West Point hospital for four months.

Another close call came at Christmastime in 1826. Davis and some other Southerners—in general, he disliked the sober and studious Northern boys—thought that Christmas would not be complete without a good old eggnog party. On Christmas Eve, Davis was one of the cadets who sneaked off to town to buy the whiskey and eggs. By one in the morning the mixing had started. Davis kept sampling the stuff to make sure it was up to the good old Southern standard. Perhaps this is the reason he left the party early. At any rate, about four in the morning Captain Hitchcock heard the noise in the party room. He entered the crowded room and started to look for liquor. Suddenly, Jefferson Davis burst in with a loud warning: "Boys, put away that grog! Captain Hitchcock is coming!"

The captain, of course, was already in the room. The embarrassed Davis heard him bark orders. Everyone who did not belong there was to return to his room and go to bed. By this time Davis was probably tipsy enough to go to sleep without orders. Anyhow, he did just as directed.

The next morning he learned what had happened. The "eggnog riot" remains one of the worst blots on West Point's history. The drunken cadets tried to force Hitchcock from the room. He called for help. Picking up clubs and whatever was handy, the cadets battled the officers out of the building and back into their own quarters. The court-martial that followed expelled nineteen cadets.

But Jefferson Davis was not among them. By a strange piece of luck, he was probably saved because he had started partying too early. He had had no part in the riot. He had not even been seen drinking.

Cadet Jefferson F. Davis managed to get through his four years of studies at West Point. He graduated with his class in the spring of 1828. Except for a near-record number of demerits, he had not distinguished himself. He graduated twenty-third in a class of thirty-three.

It should be noted that the following year a cadet named Robert E. Lee graduated second in his class while setting a West Point record—not a single demerit in four years.

CHAPTER THREE

Knox

Jefferson Davis—he dropped the Finis after West Point—was now twenty years old. He was a second lieutenant in the United States Army. Just under six feet, he appeared taller because of his slender body and very straight posture. He held his head up with the pride of an army officer and a Southern gentleman.

After West Point, Davis was due a long leave of absence to visit his family. In his case, the leave was unusually long. He asked that his vacation last until the end of 1828. For one thing, he hadn't been home in five years. For another, he wanted to avoid the malaria season in Mississippi. His request was granted. He spent some time in Lexington, Kentucky, his old college town. When it was safe to go farther south, he went to Rosemont, his boyhood home in Woodville, Mississippi. There he had a long visit with his mother and other nearby relatives.

At Rosemont, Davis finally joined up with James Pemberton, the African American left as a slave to him by his father. Davis and Pemberton had known each other as children. Years before, Pemberton had chosen Jefferson as the Davis child he most wanted as a future owner. Pemberton soon became a trusted servant and, in a way, a friend. For nearly twenty years, James Pemberton would be Davis's right-hand man. He would one day be offered his freedom when his master died.

From Rosemont, Davis and his new servant went up the Mississippi to Davis Bend. The year before, a storm had leveled the area and done much damage. Buildings had been rebuilt. Joseph Davis called his new mansion The Hurricane. It was surrounded by camellias and rose gardens, magnolia trees, and oaks hung with Spanish moss. Inside were room after room filled with French furniture, sparkling chandeliers, and row upon row of books. Black slaves obeyed every wish of Joseph Davis and his frail, obedient wife, Eliza.

At the end of the year, young Lieutenant Davis reported to Jefferson Barracks in Missouri. The post was a good one. People in nearby St. Louis invited the handsome young officers to parties and dances. Dancing had been part of the program of studies at West Point. Now Davis had a chance to show off his skill with the bewitching young beauties of the border town.

But such a life was not to last. In the spring of 1829, Davis was sent to a lonely army post in Michigan Territory. For four years he was to serve in what is now the state of Wisconsin, with some time spent in Illinois, Iowa, and Minnesota. The soldiers were there to enforce the law of the United States in the territory and to keep the settlers safe from raids by Native Americans whose lands had been taken over. Most of the Native Americans whom Davis saw, however, were peaceful traders. Only a few times did real trouble occur. Once Davis and a few soldiers were chased down a river by a larger group of American Indians. Both the soldiers and their pursuers were in canoes. Davis would probably have been killed if he hadn't managed to make a sail out of a blanket and speed away.

Much of Davis's time was spent on jobs he had never been trained for at West Point. Wisconsin was so thinly settled that the army couldn't simply buy logs and lumber to build forts. One of Davis's first assignments was to take a group of soldiers over a hundred miles up the Yellow River to cut logs, then float them down the river to a fort. During the winter of 1831-32, he was sent to build a sawmill in the wilderness. Unusually heavy snows made the work hard indeed. These difficulties, plus a poor diet and ever-damp clothing, finally got the better of the young lieutenant. He came down with pneumonia. For days, and then for weeks, he lay in bed, feverish and unable to eat. He had to give orders to his men through James Pemberton. Finally he was so thin and lifeless that Pemberton would pick him up and carry him to the window, to see how the mill was coming. But somehow he recovered. That winter Davis owed his life to the nursing skills of the faithful Pemberton.

In 1831 a new commander came to Fort Crawford, a post near the spot where the Wisconsin River runs into the Mississippi. This was Colonel Zachary Taylor, a man who would become very important in Davis's life. Taylor was an "old Indian fighter" of the type later made famous by movies in the early and mid-twentieth century. He was rugged, blunt, honest, and careless about his dress. He was also fearless, fair, and beloved by his men. The troops called him Old Rough and Ready. Taylor liked Davis at once and before long made him his assistant. He also gave Davis a long furlough, or leave of absence, in the summer of 1832.

Davis spent much of his furlough with his brother Joseph at The Hurricane. The twenty-four-year-old wanted to talk about his future. He was barely satisfied with army life. The pay was low. Promotions were slow. He had gone to West Point and stayed there mainly to please Joseph. But now, did he really want to spend the rest of his life in lonely frontier posts? Wouldn't that mean to end up without the money to marry and then to live in any kind of style? What did Joseph think?

Besides, there were other opportunities in life. The railroads were just getting started in Mississippi. Railroads would need engineers, and Davis had some engineering training. That was a good future, wasn't it? But Joseph had his doubts. Stay in the army, he said. Later he wrote Jefferson, "Of this Railroad I have no high opinion and, as you know, have always regarded it as a failure sooner or later."

When Davis returned to duty, he found some action at last. The Black Hawk War was just ending.

Black Hawk, a chief of the Sauk tribe, had been threatening trouble for years. As so often on the frontier, the conflict involved land and disputed treaties. Black Hawk wanted to reoccupy some lands he believed had been unjustly taken from the Sauk and Fox peoples. Black Hawk had decided to stand up and fight for the rights of his people. A local militia, or citizen army, had been formed to assist the U.S. troops. (The young Abe Lincoln served a short time in the Black Hawk War as captain of sixty-eight ragtag volunteers. But there is no record that he and Davis ever met.)

Black Hawk was a reasonable man. The regular army commanders, used to dealing with Native Americans, could probably have settled the differences in a peaceful way. But the militia got out of hand. Farm boys, out for what was then called some "Injun fightin'," could not be controlled. The small Black Hawk War turned into a massacre of Sauk and Fox women and children. Davis and most thoughtful officers were embarrassed about the whole affair. Davis later said that if the Black Hawk War had a hero, it was Black Hawk himself.

At last Black Hawk was captured. Davis was the officer assigned to take the chief and about forty followers down the Mississippi to jail. Black Hawk later wrote in his autobiography, "We started for Jefferson Barracks in a steamboat under the charge of a young war chief who treated us all with much kindness. He is a good and brave young chief with whose conduct I was very much pleased."

Soon someone else would be "very much pleased" with the young officer—but in a very different way. At this time Colonel Zachary Taylor's family joined Taylor at Fort Crawford. One night Jefferson Davis was invited to dinner. According to one story, the door was opened by Sarah Knox Taylor herself.

Knox, as her family called her, was then eighteen. An old portrait—this was before photography—shows a girl with a small waist and large, liquid eyes in a friendly, open face. Her long dark hair is parted in the middle and hangs down front and back, with the tips curled. Written reports say the gray-eyed Knox was very bright and quick, fun to be with, in short, "lovely and lovable."

Certainly Jefferson Davis thought so. Her parents soon saw what was happening between the two. They failed to nip young love in the bud, but they stepped in to prevent its full flowering. Zachary Taylor told Davis that he would never, never allow his daughter to marry an army man. Margaret Taylor, better than her husband, knew what the life of an army wife was like. She had worried herself sick every time her husband marched off into battle. The Taylors had been separated for long periods of time. They had never had enough money. Two daughters had been lost to disease in the Louisiana fever country. Now an older daughter was trying to make the best of a military marriage in the wilds of Minnesota. No, the affair could not go on. Davis was forbidden to enter the Taylor house or ever see Knox again.

But Jeff and Knox found secret ways to meet. She would take her young brother and sister out walking, then "accidentally" meet Jeff and send the children off to play. Or they would meet at

Sarah Knox Taylor was eighteen years old when Jefferson Davis met her. Their marriage was opposed by her parents.

the house of a friend. Colonel Taylor and his wife probably guessed that the two were secretly engaged. At any rate, Jefferson Davis suddenly found himself transferred to another unit and then assigned to a wilderness outpost in Arkansas Territory.

Except for writing and reading love letters, Davis found Arkansas miserable. "Fun" was wolf fights, horse fights, bison hunting, and endless games of poker. There were not many American Indians around, so he was not involved in any battles. The commanders tried to add interest to life by being strict and exact about every detail of military life. Over and over, Davis felt his pride injured by correction for small details he thought unimportant. Finally he had had enough of the make-work and boredom. One morning he failed to get out of bed for formation. Moreover, he talked back when questioned by Major Richard B. Mason. For this Jefferson Davis found himself court-martialed in the spring of 1835.

The court-martial took place in Memphis, Tennessee. It lasted six days. As at West Point, Davis served as his own lawyer. He tried to turn the tables on Major Mason. The major had treated him in an insulting way, he said. Davis spoke well, to the point, and at great length. He told the court that he had been asked to endure more than could ever be "required of a Gentleman."

On March 15, 1835, Davis was found not guilty—but he had had enough of the army. He immediately used his furlough time to visit Joseph at The Hurricane again. This time Joseph did not argue with his younger brother. Jeff's army career was over; that was certain. Now Joseph offered Jefferson eight hundred acres at Davis Bend to clear for a plantation of his own. The valuable land would be free. The slaves to do the work could be paid for over several years.

Davis was overjoyed. The life of a planter! Why not? Also, if he resigned from the army, Knox's parents could no longer object to her marrying a soldier. This thought made him proceed with a letter of resignation.

But Colonel and Mrs. Zachary Taylor still opposed the marriage. This time they didn't like Knox's living in lower Mississippi. Two of their children had died in the same area. They would not risk another.

Knox had turned twenty-one just before Jefferson's court-martial. She was now free to marry whomever she wanted, regardless of her parents' thoughts on the matter. Letters between the two lovers went back and forth at a furious rate. Soon Knox had a plan: She would visit an aunt who lived near Louisville, Kentucky. Jeff could come there and make her his bride at last.

Jefferson Davis and Sarah Knox Taylor were married in Kentucky on June 17, 1835. He was just twenty-seven, she twenty-one. Her parents did not approve of the wedding and did not attend. They did, however, send her some money for bridal expenses. Knox felt sure they would forget their fears and soon be treating Jeff like a son.

Right after the wedding, the couple left by steamboat for The Hurricane at Davis Bend in Mississippi. Joseph and Eliza welcomed Knox with open arms. Jefferson and Knox seemed an ideal couple. Excited and very much in love with each other, they were entering a life filled with rich opportunities. Jeff spent most of his days with James Pemberton, supervising slaves as they began clearing land. In the evenings he and Knox enjoyed the life of the favored few at The Hurricane. Both felt caught up in a rising tide of happiness. On August 11, Knox wrote a cheerful letter to her parents up North at Fort Crawford. She ended it, "Do not make yourself uneasy about me; the country is quite healthy."

A few days later, both Knox and Jeff began to feel unwell. A short rest, they thought, would do them both good. Jefferson decided it was a good time to take Knox down into Louisiana to meet his favorite sister, Anna Smith. But when they arrived at St. Francisville, Louisiana, they were looking even worse. Anna Smith thought they were very sick indeed. She put them to bed in separate rooms. She gave them the usual medicines and called a doctor and nurse. But their fevers rose. Their faces grew moist and strained. (The disease was probably malaria, but could have been yellow fever.) Their minds began to drift in and out, losing touch with reality and then taking hold once again.

So that neither would know just how ill the other really was, Anna insisted that they stay apart. But on September 15, Jeff floated into a wakeful moment to hear Knox singing. The song was "Fairy Bells,"one of their favorites. He got out of bed and stumbled to her room. Her eyes were open, but she did not know who he was. Jeff felt that Death was standing at his side.

Tradition says that she died in his arms. They had been married not quite three months.

CHAPTER FOUR

Varina

For days Jefferson Davis's own life hung in the balance. One morning he would be a little better, the next morning worse. But at last the crisis passed. Improvement set in. By the end of a month he was able to return to Davis Bend, even if James Pemberton did have to carry him onto the steamboat. Back at The Hurricane, his physical health slowly came back.

His mental health was another thing. Knox was now gone for good, and Jefferson Davis was a changed man. Knox was ever present in his head, yet ever absent from his side. Davis was the kind of man who seldom admitted a mistake, but in this case he must have punished himself severely. Why had he ever brought his bride to lower Mississippi during the fever season? He had known the chances. After all, right after West Point he had had his leave extended because of the danger. He had wanted to avoid the fever season in Mississippi. But after years of waiting for Knox, he just hadn't been able to wait any longer. Now he suffered sleepless nights and troubled days. One story says that years later he found one of Knox's slippers in an old suitcase. He fainted at the sight.

To escape memories of Knox at The Hurricane, Davis decided to take a long vacation. He and James Pemberton left for New Orleans, then for Cuba. In the spring he returned to Davis Bend to take up his new life as a planter. He was not to leave the area for more than two years. The carefree cadet and dashing young lieutenant now seemed to be a man in hiding.

Davis, Pemberton, and ten slaves set themselves to the task of turning land covered with burned stumps and briers into cotton fields. Pemberton proved to be an excellent overseer. This made it easier for Davis, who now had to learn how to manage slaves instead of soldiers.

In dealing with slaves, Davis had another model—his brother

Joseph. Never for a moment did Joseph Davis—or Jefferson Davis either—believe that black people were the equals of white people. But for the Old South, the Davis plantations were models of race relations. Very seldom if ever was a slave whipped. There was no slave jail to be seen. Blacks who broke the rules had to face a jury of other—and usually older—black people. A dentist came for yearly checkups, and doctors were called for the sick. The slaves lived in two-room whitewashed cabins with fireplaces. Although on some plantations the slaves lived on corn meal, salt pork, and molasses, the Davis slaves also had coffee, sugar, flour, and milk. They had their own garden plots, peach trees, and chicken coops. Corn for the chickens was free. Nearby planters sometimes wondered about the way Joseph Davis treated his black property. "Mr. Davis's free Negroes," they scoffed.

There were laws in many parts of the South against such things as arming slaves or teaching them to read. The Davis slaves, however, were given guns to go hunting. Joseph Davis thought that any slave who *could* learn *should* learn. Benjamin T. Montgomery is a good example. When Joseph bought him, Ben Montgomery could read and write well. Joseph gave him the free run of his library. Although he remained a slave, Montgomery was allowed to open a little store at Davis Bend, dealing with whites and blacks alike. Montgomery's store was entirely his own independent operation. His two sons, Isaiah and Thornton, became what today would be called business managers. (Two years after the Civil War, in fact, the Montgomerys bought The Hurricane for $300,000. "We just barely had an idea of what slave life was," Isaiah said of his youth.)

If anything, Jefferson's treatment of slaves was even better than Joseph's. This was because Jefferson had fewer of them (forty by 1840 and seventy-four by 1845). Davis was proud that he knew each slave well. He even knew the names of the babies of his enslaved African Americans. A slave birth or wedding brought presents or a feast. When Davis went to the slave quarters, the children called him "Marse Jeff" and clung to his legs. Davis never broke up a family; he never even sold a slave. He went out of his way to see that elderly slaves lived in comfort.

Still, it should be said again that Jefferson Davis never considered any black person his equal. To him, slaves were a separate and inferior kind of people whose happiness depended on the care and love their good Christian owners gave them.

Clearing land and raising cotton took most of Davis's time. But not all. He designed a house for himself and Pemberton. Because he was tall, the windows were high. For summer breezes he made the doors six feet wide. The name seemed a natural one: Brierfield. There he and Pemberton would sit down after a day's work and go over plans for the next. Though Pemberton was Jim to most, he was always James to Jefferson Davis. This slave owner believed that to call a slave a nickname was a sign of disrespect. When they parted company, James always carried a fine cigar.

Davis ate most of his dinners and spent most of his evenings at The Hurricane. Joseph's mansion had a separate library, a large building built like a Greek temple. To keep Knox from his mind, Jefferson began to read as he never had before. History, government, novels, poetry—it was a second education. He especially liked poetry, and soon he could recite pages of it from memory. Shakespeare and the Bible he read over and over. In the future he would season his speeches with quotations. At "name the author" games he would have no master.

In the fall of 1837, after two years of mourning the death of Knox, Davis felt enough like his old self to want a change of scene. That winter he took his first vacation in a long time. First he traveled to New York City. Then he went to Washington, D.C. An old Transylvania friend, George W. Jones, now represented Iowa Territory in the Congress. Jones showed Davis the inner workings of the national government. He also introduced him to a congressman Davis liked at once: Franklin Pierce of New Hampshire. (Pierce, like Zachary Taylor, would later be a U.S. President.) The high point of the Washington trip was a breakfast Pierce arranged with President Martin Van Buren. Jefferson Davis expected that the President would talk learnedly of politics and government. He was disappointed. Instead, Van Buren's chief interest seemed to be where Davis had bought his handsome Southern boots.

The trip to Washington aroused a new interest in Jefferson Davis: good government. Back at Davis Bend, he buried himself in Joseph's library for hours at a time. In Washington he had seen the Senate and House in action. *The National Intelligencer* and *Congressional Globe*, which Joseph read eagerly, reprinted all important speeches in Congress. Joseph and Jefferson now spent their evenings reading and discussing newspapers and books. The subject was almost always politics. Little by little, Jefferson began to go with Joseph to political meetings. Both men, like their father Samuel before them, were eager Democrats.

In 1843 the Democratic candidate for Warren County's seat in the state legislature suddenly dropped out of the race. Jefferson Davis had been noticed as an educated man and thoughtful speaker. Now the county leaders needed a replacement candidate in a hurry. The election was about a week away. Did Davis want to step in?

The chance to enter politics finally drew Jefferson Davis out of his eight-year shell. But his chance to win the election was small indeed. At the time the two main political parties were the Democrats and the Whigs. In Warren County, the Whig party nearly always won. Still, Davis did what he could in the few days before the election. He got 43 percent of the vote. This was a good showing for a Democrat in Warren County. It brought him to the attention of state Democratic leaders.

The fall election was over, but the year 1843 held one more surprise for Jefferson Davis. That was the year he met Varina Anne Howell of Natchez, Mississippi.

Joseph Davis liked to celebrate the Christmas season at The Hurricane in a big way. The welcome mat was always out for relatives, friends, and even for relatives of friends. Guests often arrived in early December and stayed into January. So it was that in 1843 Joseph invited Varina Howell, the daughter of a good friend, William B. Howell of Natchez.

Her name was pronounced Va-REE-na. She was seventeen years old. At five foot seven inches, she was tall for a girl at the time. She had a good figure and very dark hair worn in a swirl on top of her head. Her large eyes, set in a lively face, were so dark brown as to be almost black.

Varina had other attractions for Jefferson Davis. Her mind was quick. Her words had bite. Her education was unusual for a girl in the 1840s. She had gone to a school in Philadelphia for two terms, but most of her education had come from a private tutor, Judge George Winchester. A Massachusetts man, Judge Winchester had retired to the beautiful Natchez bluffs overlooking the Mississippi. He enjoyed teaching languages and literature. Amazed at Varina's love of learning, he had always treated her as an adult. She called him Great Heart, in the same loving way that she called her host at The Hurricane Uncle Joe. For years Joseph Davis had been a frequent guest at the Howells' handsome home in Natchez.

Varina's winter trip in 1843 was a great new experience for her. Away from home and her parents, she came up the Mississippi in the finest new steamboat on the river, the *Magnolia*. She called it a "floating palace." Her surprise continued as she arrived at The Hurricane. The Greek temple of a library was enough to amaze anyone. Then there were the grounds—the fountains, statues, fruit trees, and flower beds. Inside the huge house she found a new thrill—running water, uncommon at the time. (Slaves pumped water into an attic tank every morning, from which it moved through pipes to rooms below.) Then of course there were the attentions of Uncle Joe's handsome younger brother, Jefferson. That Jefferson was twice her age perhaps added to the tingle of excitement.

Varina's intelligence and insight can be seen in a letter written to her mother right after her first meeting with Jefferson Davis. "He impresses me," she wrote, "as a remarkable kind of man, but of uncertain temper, and has a way of taking for granted that everybody agrees with him when he expresses an opinion, which offends me." (That remark was a bull's-eye judgment. Jefferson Davis was hardly without faults. He was a proud man who tended to place himself above others. His pride made him overly sensitive to criticism. And—as Varina had quickly noted—he could never understand why anyone might disagree with him. Facts were facts, he thought. Logic was logic. When he put facts and logic together and a person was still not persuaded . . . well, the person was either stupid or dishonest.)

"Yet," Varina's letter went on, "he is most agreeable, and has a particularly sweet voice and a winning manner." She was soon

When Jefferson Davis met Varina Anne Howell in 1843, he was 35 years old and she was 17.

learning more about that "winning manner," day after day. Jefferson showed her Joseph's stable of thirty fine horses. Which one did she want to ride? Together they toured the two plantations, The Hurricane and Brierfield. When they came to an open stretch of land, they would race their horses. Varina always ended up laughing and last. But Jefferson was pleased at the way she could keep up, in spite of the sidesaddle that women used at the time. She thought Jefferson's own house interesting but odd. When she sat down, the windows were too high to see out of. When he opened one of the wide doors, "the side of the house seemed to be taken down." On rainy afternoons, they would retreat to the music room at The Hurricane. Varina would play the piano as Jefferson sang songs in his full, rich voice.

In the evenings, Joseph and Jefferson would usually go into Joseph's study. There they would read the papers and talk politics. Varina would sit in the tea room with Eliza and the other women. She hated to pass time with needlework and chitchat while the men were discussing BIG IDEAS. But sooner or later the men's eyes would grow tired in the lantern light. Varina would be called in to read aloud. Both men were amazed at the way she could toss off a French phrase and handle Latin like a native language. Great Heart had done his job well.

Judge Winchester had also kept Varina on top of current events. But like her family, she was a Whig—and proud of it. She liked to argue, and she could fight like a cat. Jefferson loved it. "Would you believe it," Varina wrote her mother, "he is refined and cultivated and yet he is a Democrat." (At the time, most of the rich and refined were also Whigs.)

She was seventeen, he was thirty-five. Yet this difference was as nothing between two people who liked many of the same things—even the same poems. By Christmas Day, even the slaves were whispering about the growing romance. No one who saw them together could fail to see it. When Varina finally left, probably in early February, the whispers were of marriage. Jefferson wanted to call on Margaret and William Howell as soon as possible. He would formally ask their permission to marry Varina.

But Varina cautioned against this action. She knew she had more of a problem than Jefferson imagined. Margaret Howell did not take her daughter's news with great joy. Everything she'd heard about Jefferson Davis pleased her, but... He was a Democrat, not a Whig. He was a Baptist, not an Episcopalian. He was from a newly rich family, while Varina's family had long been wealthy and powerful. (Her grandfather had been an eight-year governor of New Jersey.) And Jefferson Davis had not only been married once, but was twice Varina's age. Why, Jefferson Davis was only two years younger than Margaret Howell herself!

Meanwhile, love letters flew back and forth. Written in the flowery style of the time, some of these letters still exist. "My own dearest Varina," Jefferson would begin. "Since you left I have found the house particularly dull. . . . I believe everybody thinks of you, as soon as they see me, or . . . when I enter the rooms in which we were together. . . . But why shall I not come to see you?" He would end in French: "Bon soir, ma chere ange" (Good night, my dear angel).

Varina did not let her beloved "Jeffers" come to meet her parents until the coast was clear. This happened some time in March 1844. She wrote that Judge Winchester, her dear Great Heart, had helped her win the day. Now her parents agreed to the marriage. Jefferson, in turn, had nothing but praise for "my dear friend the Judge. . . . He would have a poor opinion, I doubt not, of any man who having an opportunity to know you would not love you."

When Jefferson finally made his formal call on the Howells, Varina's clear coast made for smooth sailing. Jefferson Davis carried a good impression as easily as he carried his tailored clothes. He won the Howells over completely. The engagement was announced in the proper way. The marriage itself, however, did not take place for nearly a year. There were at least three reasons for this.

First, Davis spent much of 1844 working for the Democratic party. A presidential election was coming up. From the Tennessee border to the Gulf of Mexico, from the Alabama line to the Mississippi River, Davis toured the state making speeches. He addressed gatherings large and small. Everywhere he went he preached the Southern Democrats' message. Admit Texas as a state. Get rid of tariffs, the taxes on goods imported from other countries. Expand U.S. claims in the Northwest. Nominate for

President a man who would spread the message and win. (And in fact this is just what happened. A Southern Democrat, James K. Polk, won the 1844 election with Mississippi's help.)

Second, Varina kept coming down with attacks of some mysterious disease. Perhaps it was just nerves. At any rate she was ill enough to keep pushing a wedding date further into the future. This may have had something to do with the third reason, differences between the couple themselves. For her time, Varina was a strong-minded woman. She wanted not only Jefferson but a say in their life together. For instance, she had her doubts about living at Davis Bend. How could they live at The Hurricane? It would be hard. Joseph ran everything there and would run her life as well. Varina was just not cut out to be a spineless wife like Joseph's frail Eliza. Could they live at Brierfield? Perhaps. But Jefferson's odd house was a real comedown from the stately Howell mansion in Natchez.

The Briars, birthplace of Varina Anne Howell, in Natchez, Mississippi. Here she and Jefferson Davis were married.

But finally all was in order. Polk was elected President. Varina's health improved. The differences were settled. Jefferson Davis and eighteen-year-old Varina Anne Howell were married in Natchez on February 16, 1845.

The honeymoon started in a strange way. The first stop was the home of Jeff's sister Anna in St. Francisville, Louisiana. There Jefferson took Varina to the grave of his first wife, Knox. Although Varina later wrote many pages about their life together, she never even hinted at her feelings as she, the second wife, stood silently above the body of wife number one. At least the rest of the trip went better. At Rosemont, Varina enjoyed meeting Jeff's mother, then in her eighties. After that it was off to the luxurious St. Charles Hotel in New Orleans. It was a lush, romantic setting for a loving, romantic couple. They stayed six weeks.

Jefferson and Varina Davis. The newly married couple returned to Brierfield after their honeymoon in New Orleans.

Back at Brierfield, Jeff and Varina settled down to a life of expanding cotton fields and hopes. Varina, though feeling "loving but useless" at times, tried hard to fill the role of a planter's wife. She learned how to nurse sick slaves and do countless other chores.

As he turned thirty-seven, Jefferson Davis probably felt that the puzzle pieces of life were coming together at last. After a false start in the army, he now had a clear road ahead as a planter. After losing his first bride, he now had another who made him feel blissfully young, fully alive. As he and Varina rode through their acres in the soft Mississippi twilight, they must have felt that just around every corner were years of secure success. He was happy. Things seemed right.

CHAPTER FIVE

Washington and War

The peaceful life of the Brierfield planter was not to last long. A little over a month after his thirty-seventh birthday, a state Democratic convention chose Jefferson Davis as a candidate for the House of Representatives in Washington, D.C. Mississippi congressmen were then elected "at large" by all state voters, not in individual districts as today.

Had he worked for his own nomination? In a way, yes. Certainly, he had done nothing to oppose it. At the time, it was common for political hopefuls to do all they could behind the scenes, then sit back and wait to be "called" by party leaders for the office. Running for Congress in no way meant that the master of Brierfield was giving up his career as a planter. In the 1840s, many men—Abraham Lincoln among them—served a term or two in Congress, then returned to their own careers. Serving in Washington was hardly a year-round job. Congressmen had most of the summer and fall to spend at home. Besides, Davis knew that James Pemberton, with brother Joseph looking on, could keep Brierfield on track while he was away.

So once again Jefferson Davis went out on the campaign trail—this time on his own behalf. Once again he traveled hundreds of miles by horse, coach, and steamboat to address the voters. Before the age of radio and television—before microphones and loudspeakers—there was only one way to campaign: Get out there and speak to people in range of your voice. If you were lucky, your remarks might be carried in a local newspaper.

Voters who heard Jefferson Davis heard a very different kind of politician. No wild waving of the arms. No promises without a plan to keep them. No four-hour speeches. Instead the voters heard a calm, pleasant voice coming from a handsome man who looked intelligent and certainly knew what he was talking about. At the same time, the voters sensed that Jefferson Davis somehow thought himself superior, in no way a "man of the people."

Varina Davis later said that her husband "did not know the arts of the politician." Some of his advisers at the time wanted him to be a more forceful speaker. Why not gesture and shout and threaten the end of the world if not elected? Jefferson Davis went on speaking in the way he thought best. He had the facts behind him, the logic behind him, and he knew that he was right. He didn't need to kiss all the babies in sight or slap all the backs he could find.

As a Democrat in a state where Democrats outnumbered Whigs, Davis was expected to win. But in the November elections, he wasn't expected to win with many votes to spare. Yet here was clearly a young politician on his way up.

He won the election with votes to spare.

Left behind at Davis Bend, Varina had not had an easy time during Jeff's political campaign. It hadn't seemed right for the nineteen-year-old Varina to stay at Brierfield without him, so she had moved to The Hurricane. Uncle Joe's Christmas in 1843 had seemed wonderful to her, but now things were different. Joseph Davis made all the decisions. His wife Eliza always agreed. Then there was Amanda, a Davis sister who had just lost her husband and moved in with seven children. Amanda had a sharp tongue. Both she and Eliza were mature women. To them, young Jeff's much younger bride was just a girl. Varina probably thought that going to Washington, D.C., would be a big change for the better.

In late November 1845, Jefferson and Varina Davis left for Washington. At the time, the one railroad in Mississippi went only halfway through the state. The new congressman and his wife took a steamboat up the Mississippi and then eastward on the Ohio River. December cold came early in 1845, and blocks of ice hitting the boat made it hard to sleep. Before long the ice had not only stopped the boat but surrounded it. The steamship captain waited day after day for the ice to break. No luck. After a week, the passengers were taken off in a much smaller boat and dropped off at the nearest town.

Snow and ice covered the roads. The only way east was by horse-drawn sleigh. Riding in the open sleigh, Varina perched on a trunk with Jefferson and a much older Mississippi congressman seated together. The sleigh slipped from side to side. The Ohio weather grew colder. The next jolt, they kept feeling, might tip the sled over. Finally the sleigh did go over, sending passengers, boxes, trunks, and suitcases down a twenty-foot bank. But at last the party reached Wheeling, Virginia (now West Virginia). Varina had a cut on her head. Jeff's feet were frozen. The old congressman had a painful broken rib.

The rest of the trip, mostly by stagecoach, was little better. The coach, too, bounced and slipped on the icy roads. The passengers were thrown around like salt in a shaker. All got bruises. The three-week trip finally ended at the door of the National Hotel in Washington. Varina and the two congressmen, dirty, tired, and ailing, felt out of place in the magnificent lobby.

The Capitol, Washington, D.C. When Jefferson and Varina Davis arrived in the city, the building had not been completed.

Washington was then a capital city of fewer than 30,000 people. It was a city of some splendor, but also of outhouses and open sewers. Only one street was paved. Only the central portion of the Capitol Building had been built. It was topped by a temporary wooden dome.

Congressmen in those days usually did not own or rent their own homes in Washington, D.C. Instead, they stayed in boardinghouses. Part of the boardinghouse life was what was called a congressional mess. A mess was a group of people who regularly took their meals together. In a way, the messes were like social clubs. There, groups of like-minded congressmen ate and talked and swapped stories. There the wives made friends. Varina and Jefferson soon moved into Mrs. Potter's boardinghouse and found themselves in a comfortable mess.

There was a lot going on in Washington during the winter of 1845-46. Plays, dances, dinners, parties—all were there for the asking. But Jefferson Davis was never a man who liked events that were purely social. And Varina, at nineteen, tended to hold back. They did attend White House receptions given by President and Mrs. Polk. They also found time for the National Exposition of 1845. This was a sort of huge state fair on a national scale. In one building Varina and Jefferson gazed in astonishment at a new machine that could actually sew two pieces of cloth together. A "sewing jenny," Varina called it. A short time later they found themselves looking at the first telegraph. A man seated in a little booth could send and receive messages on a wire that ran clear to Baltimore, Maryland. Varina paid a quarter to learn that the weather in Baltimore was fine. But she didn't believe a thing. "I think it is a trick," she noted in a letter.

Varina's letters were soon complaining that Jefferson was working too hard. Unable to sleep, he often sat at his desk till two or three in the morning. His red eyes, she thought, were a sign of poor health. She did what she could to lighten his load. Today congressmen have large staffs to help them, but Varina was a staff of one. Over and over and over, she copied his letters and speeches to send back to Mississippi. She did research. She opened mail and kept the files. On rare days when she had nothing to do, her favorite place was the gallery of the U.S. Senate.

U.S. Senator John C. Calhoun of South Carolina.

U.S. Senator Henry Clay of Kentucky.

This was the great age of the Senate, when some of its long-time members were better known than passing presidents. Now Varina Davis could see and hear the men she had been reading about for years: Daniel Webster of Massachusetts; John C. Calhoun of South Carolina; and between them in both geography and politics, the great man of compromise, Senator Henry Clay of Kentucky.

One of the burning issues of the day was the future expansion of the United States. In the Pacific Northwest, the huge area called Oregon Country was up for grabs. It included what are now Oregon, Washington, Idaho, and parts of Montana, Wyoming, and Canada. In the early 1800s, the Oregon wilderness had been claimed by Great Britain, Russia, Spain, and the United States. By 1818, it was jointly occupied by Great Britain and the United States. But now some in Washington wanted to claim the Oregon Country completely, all the way north to Russian Alaska. They believed that if they had to fight the British to get it, then they would fight the British. It was much the same in the Southwest. The present states of New Mexico, Arizona, California, Nevada, Utah, and parts of Colorado and Wyoming—all were part of Mexico. A war with Mexico just might be worth the winnings.

Davis's first important speech in Congress concerned the Oregon Country. Then as now, freshmen congressmen were supposed to be seen and not heard. But Davis thought the issue too important to ignore. Soon after he rose to speak, it was clear that he had done his homework well. Although his party generally favored grabbing all of the Oregon Country, Davis favored a peaceful deal with the British. He pointed out that every reason given for wanting the Oregon Country could be satisfied with just the southern portion. His military experience made him doubtful about sending and supplying an army so far away. His pleasant voice and calm, factual reasoning impressed his listeners. (And today, the western boundary between the United States and Canada is just where Davis thought it should be.)

The most respected person in the House at this time was John Quincy Adams of Massachusetts. After serving as the sixth U.S. President, Adams had done an unheard of thing. He had gone back to Washington as a congressman. Now he was old and hard of hearing. When a new member rose to speak, Adams would move his chair so that he could hear. If he liked what he heard, he would stay to listen. If he disliked the man or the message, he would never listen again. In this case Adams liked what he heard. "That young man, gentlemen, is no ordinary man," he remarked. "Mind me, he will make his mark yet. He will go far."

As for the Southwest, however, Davis had other ideas. Texas had become a state shortly before Davis entered the House. The trouble was that the border between Texas and Mexico had never been agreed to. The United States claimed the border was at the Rio Grande. The Mexicans claimed the border was farther north at the Nueces River.

In 1846 President James Knox Polk sent a force under General Zachary Taylor south from the Nueces River to the Rio Grande. The Mexicans moved troops northward across the Rio Grande. A few small battles were fought on the land between the two rivers, land claimed by both sides. This allowed Polk to claim that American blood had been spilled on American soil. He called for war. Congress agreed and declared war on Mexico.

Many Northerners opposed the war. They saw it as a scheme by Southern slave owners to add more slave states to the Union.

(A young Illinois congressman named Abraham Lincoln was bitterly against the Mexican War.) But Jefferson Davis, like most Southerners, thought the advantages of the war outweighed the risks. With his military background, Davis even thought at once of leaving his seat in the House for a short, glorious fight.

Varina now declared a war of her own. Jefferson would *not* go, she stated. It was the first open break in their marriage. With his trouble sleeping, his eye infections, and his frequent earaches, Jefferson was really in poor health. Moreover, Varina knew that her younger brother, Joseph Davis Howell, had signed up as a private. At six feet seven inches, brother Joe would make a tall target for Mexican rifles. Wasn't it too much to ask of her, to risk a brother and husband, too? Jefferson made Varina some kind of promise that he would not volunteer. He did not, however, say what he would do if "called" to serve.

The call came in late June 1846. Davis was asked to command the First Mississippi Volunteers with the rank of colonel. He would serve under his old hero and former father-in-law, Zachary Taylor. The year before, Davis had met Old Rough and Ready for the first time in ten years. Taylor now had no bad feelings toward his former son-in-law. Knox's death had been an accident, nobody's fault. After all, the marriage and the move to Mississippi had been just what Knox wanted to do.

After resigning from Congress in June 1846, Davis left Washington on July 4 for war. He took his wife to The Hurricane, then joined his unit near New Orleans. It was "like death to see him go," Varina told friends. Under his command were nearly a thousand crack Mississippi riflemen. Davis had made a deal with the army that his men would have modern rifles, not old-fashioned muskets. The First Mississippi Volunteers soon became known as the Mississippi Rifles.

Today, the Mexican War seems made for the movie screen. The Mississippi Rifles wore big black hats, white pants, and red shirts. The pride of the opposing army was the Mexican Lancers. Mounted on fine horses, these cavalrymen went into battle like medieval knights. Their lances sparkled in the hot Mexican sun. Huge colored feathers waved atop polished brass helmets. A band played behind them.

51

The Mexican Lancers. A 19th-century artist drew this picture showing the famous cavalry without their brass helmets.

The Mississippi Rifles saw their first real action in the Battle of Monterrey (a city in northeastern Mexico). With sword waving high, Davis led his troops in the charge. Bullets screamed past his ears. He helped capture a fort and then entered the city itself. It was a street-by-street battle. Davis's coolness and courage under fire amazed his soldiers. Joseph Davis Howell wrote home that "if he should tell his men to jump into a cannon's mouth they would think it all right, and would say, 'Colonel Jeff,' as they call him, 'knows best, so hurrah, boys let's go ahead.'"

Varina shuddered when she read letters like this. Such news was even worse than the numb terror of no news at all. Nor had she had an easy time at The Hurricane. Eliza and Amanda had combined criticism and false cheer to make her feel miserable. Joseph had added to her burden. Varina now learned that Jefferson's will left part of what he owned to his widowed sister, Amanda. Even worse, although Joseph had "given" Brierfield to Jefferson, no legal land transfer had ever taken place. If her husband were to die, Varina would have little.

One project that cheered Varina up was her drawing of plans for the new mansion that would someday replace Jeff's oddly designed house. But it seemed that in Joseph's mind, the new Brierfield was to be large enough to hold Amanda and all her children, too. The strain was too much for Varina. "I have cried until I am stupid," she had said. She began to sulk in her room, pleading illness. Then she left for her parents' home in Natchez, not planning to return. She wrote her husband letter after letter, begging him to come home. Her mind was gnawed by worry and fear. With Jeff in danger, she felt ill, close to death herself.

After Monterrey, Davis grew so anxious about Varina's worry that he applied for a furlough. He went to Mississippi for a short visit. At The Hurricane with Varina, he tried to smooth things out. At length, Varina agreed to stay and help James Pemberton manage Brierfield. Davis offered Pemberton his freedom if his master should die in battle. No, Pemberton replied, "Miss Varina" would need his help. James Pemberton would agree to accept his freedom only if Jefferson and Varina had both died.

Back in Mexico, Davis learned that the war had changed somewhat. Politics had interfered. General Taylor, Old Rough and Ready, was a military man, not a political one. It was thought, however, that he was a Whig. This had worried President Polk and other Democrats in Washington. With every battle, Zachary Taylor was becoming more and more of a hero. If his popularity continued to soar, the Whigs would have the perfect candidate to defeat Polk in 1848. To prevent this, most of Taylor's troops were assigned to another general, Winfield Scott. Taylor was to try to hold his ground in northern Mexico. Scott was to take his large army and drive toward Mexico City.

Now Antonio López de Santa Anna, the Mexican dictator-general, saw his chance. For the moment, he would forget about Scott. He would take his whole army and move against Taylor's reduced force. Santa Anna knew he outnumbered Taylor four to one. A great victory over the famous Taylor, Santa Anna thought, would probably end the war.

Taylor had moved his 4,700 men south of Monterrey. When Santa Anna advanced, Taylor pulled back to an estate called Buena Vista. There, in front of a small pass leading into mountains, he decided to make his stand. He could not be surrounded. The battle would be held to a small area. Taylor knew that this was the only way for a small army to fight a large one. The showdown came on February 23, 1847.

Right after the fighting started, Davis, on horseback, was clipped in the right heel by a Mexican bullet. Chips of brass spur were driven into broken pieces of bone. But he ignored the wound. On his left, a unit from Indiana gave way under enemy fire. Taylor ordered Davis to hold at all costs. Davis managed to add some of the Indiana soldiers to his ranks. He formed his troops into a huge **V** formation, with the open end toward the enemy. As the Americans tried to lie low behind rocks, the Mexican Lancers entered the **V**. Davis's sharpshooters held their fire. Had the Mexicans kept going and charged, they might well have broken through. But for some reason they stopped. The Mississippi Rifles now had the enemy in deadly cross fire. The Mexicans dropped from their horses or panicked. Their confused retreat ran right into shells fired by Taylor's artillery in the rear. The Americans had won the day. They now controlled northeastern Mexico.

In truth, the Battle of Buena Vista was a small engagement. Davis lost only thirty-nine men—a loss that might have gone unnoted in the horrible Civil War that followed. But at the time the battle was THE BIG STORY for newspapers across the United States. It made the name Jefferson Davis known to millions. From that point on, he would be the Hero of Buena Vista. Other victories by Taylor followed. In September 1847, Scott's forces occupied Mexico City. Mexico lost the war. The northern half of Mexico became part of the United States.

The Battle of Buena Vista, 1847. Because of the American victory, Davis became known as the Hero of Buena Vista.

Four months after the Battle of Buena Vista, a band burst into joyful noise on a New Orleans dock. Flags waved. Banners screamed "The Hero of Buena Vista!" Jefferson Davis, looking thin and trying to hide the pain in his heel, came down a gangplank on crutches. As he passed, women and girls threw flowers. Men made speeches, and more bands played.

Varina had not felt up to the great arrival at New Orleans. She met Jefferson at Natchez. One look at his face told her that he needed bed rest and a doctor, not more bands and speeches. But the celebration had to go on—at Natchez and then at Vicksburg, too—before she could get Jefferson back to the safe haven of Brierfield.

CHAPTER SIX

Davis Draws the Line

Once again, however, Jefferson Davis was not to stay at Brierfield. President James K. Polk offered to make him a brigadier general in the army. Governor Albert Brown of Mississippi offered to appoint him to a seat left vacant in the U.S. Senate by the death of a senator. Much to Varina's relief, Jefferson took the civilian job. He would go to the Senate.

But Varina was not wholly pleased. For months she had been doing her best by Brierfield. Now she thought that Jefferson should stay home and do his best, too. Also, her husband was hardly a healthy man. He could not put his right foot down without wincing in agony. Doctors thought another operation would be necessary to pull bits of brass from his heel. He still had trouble sleeping. A disease of the nerves called neuralgia sometimes shot needles of pain through his face. This seemed to bring back the old eye problem.

Varina had other complaints as well. The old question of the will and her rights as a wife had not been settled. Neither had the matter of their new house. How would these questions ever be decided if they went off to Washington? Since their marriage, Jefferson had been away about half the time. He seemed unable to resist the call of the army bugle or the ballot box. Varina wanted a home of her own, a husband who stayed there, and more than ever now, children. Jefferson was thirty-nine—about time he started a family, Varina thought.

The fall of 1847 was the low point in the marriage of Jefferson and Varina Davis. Their many differences hung in the air between them. Sometimes sharp words were hurled back and forth. Each accused the other of being too demanding. There was even talk of a separation. And in a way, that is just what happened. When Jefferson left for Washington on November 11, Varina was not at his side. Nor did she go to Washington the following year, for the 1848-49 Senate session. (The state legislature had by then elected him to finish the rest of the term. At the time senators were elected by state legislatures, not directly by the people.)

Alone and often in pain, Davis took a room at Gadsby's Hotel in the nation's capital. His personal troubles had made him a changed man. Even after work he could not relax. His temper had a short fuse. Often there to light the fuse was Henry S. Foote, the other senator from Mississippi and a man Davis detested. Davis considered Foote a politician without principle, a man whose opinions were formed only by the votes they might attract. One argument at Gadsby's turned into a shouting match and then a fistfight. Davis, bad heel and all, had Foote on the floor fighting off blows before friends separated them. They had hardly stood up when a remark by Foote again brought Davis on him with both fists flying.

Such behavior was not, of course, expected or accepted on the floor of the U.S. Senate. When Davis took his Senate seat on December 6, 1848, he was his old and better self again.

Well-dressed, dignified, and erect even though on crutches, the Hero of Buena Vista received a hearty welcome. He was already a nationally known figure. In the dozen years that remained before the Civil War, he would become famous as the leading Senate spokesman for Southern interests. After those dozen years, he would be the South's great hope as president of the Confederate States of America.

Davis was a hard-working, well-informed senator. His interests were not limited to the South or the defense of slavery. As a young man, he had seen the great possibilities of railroads. Now he argued for a coast-to-coast railway system. He wanted laws passed that would make it possible for a steam locomotive to go all the way from New York City to San Francisco. (This finally did happen, but only after the Civil War.)

Davis also joined the Military Affairs Committee of the Senate and, in time, became its chairman. As a military man himself, he gave good advice that other senators listened to. Another of Davis's interests was the Smithsonian Institution. He was influential in getting it started, and later he served on its board of directors. Today known mainly as a museum, the Smithsonian was then to be a center for scientific advancement. Davis was hard to entice away from his books and papers for a social event. But he was usually on hand for a scientific one.

For years and years, the champion of the Southern cause in the Senate had been John C. Calhoun of South Carolina. He was committed to slavery and the rights of the states to decide such important questions themselves. But when Davis arrived, Calhoun's energies were almost gone. He was more feeble than old. Years of effort had taken their toll. Davis never asked for the job, but Calhoun's position in the Senate soon became his. No one but Davis could plead the cause of the slave states with Calhoun's old drive and determination.

When Jefferson Davis arrived in the Senate, he again had to face the old territorial problems that had concerned him as a member of the House. The Pacific Northwest dispute had been pretty much settled by a treaty with Great Britain during the Mexican War. The British had agreed to divide the territory known as Oregon Country on a line that is now the northern border of the states of Washington, Idaho, and Montana. Few people seriously thought that slavery would ever spread into these northern regions.

The old problem in the Southwest, however, was more alive than ever before. In 1848, as a result of the Mexican War, the United States held not only Texas, but also the areas now known as New Mexico, Arizona, California, Nevada, Utah, and parts of Colorado and Wyoming. When Jefferson Davis entered the Senate, the question was what to do with all this new real estate. Would it be slave territory or free?

The question of slavery was an old one. It had troubled the nation since its founding. Some of the men at the Constitutional Convention in 1787 had refused to sign their names because the Constitution permitted slavery. Even at that time, many Americans had thought it monstrous that one human being should be allowed to own another. Benjamin Franklin's last active interest, for instance, was the abolishment of slavery. Slavery was not only wrong, many believed, it was a hideous, outdated evil.

The Constitution said nothing about slavery in new states

that might be added to the Union. But it did say that laws had to be passed by both the Senate and the House of Representatives. In the Senate, each state, regardless of its population, had two votes. This meant that as long as the number of Southern states equaled the number of Northern states, every new law would have to have the South's approval. For this reason new states were admitted to the Union in pairs, so that neither South nor North lost its equality. In 1819 the balance was eleven slaveholding states, eleven free states. Then Missouri applied for statehood. Its constitution permitted slavery. By this time the population of the fast-growing North exceeded that of the South. Many Northerners objected to the admission of still another slave state. When was it ever going to stop? Enough was enough!

The battle between Northern and Southern forces in Congress continued into the next year. In 1820 the famous Missouri Compromise was agreed to. Under the compromise, Missouri was admitted as a slave state, with Maine balancing it as a free state. More important, an imaginary line was drawn westward from the southern border of Missouri. North of this line—latitude 36° 30'—slavery was to be prohibited. Future slave states would have to be carved out of the territory south of 36° 30'. Neither North nor South really liked the terms of the bargain. But both hoped it was a way of settling the slavery question forever.

William Lloyd Garrison, journalist and abolitionist.

The North was particularly disappointed with the Missouri Compromise. The abolitionists—as those eager to abolish slavery came to be called—wanted no new slave states whatsoever. They believed that one did not compromise with evil, one stamped it out wherever it was found. In 1831 the abolitionist William Lloyd Garrison published the first issue of *The Liberator* in Boston. "I will not excuse—I will not retreat a single inch—AND I WILL BE HEARD," Garrison announced as he began to bring the outrages of slavery to the public mind. That same year Nat Turner led a slave rebellion in Virginia. More than fifty white people died and at least a hundred black people were killed in revenge before the revolt was crushed. Abolitionists pointed to the event as proof that the slaves were not the happy, satisfied workers claimed by their owners. Some abolitionists like Wendell Phillips and the

One member of the "singing Hutchinsons," a popular vocal group, dedicated this song to abolitionist Frederick Douglass.

gifted escaped slave Frederick Douglass were regularly speaking out wherever a crowd could be found.

Jefferson Davis came to the Senate when the slavery issue was again at the boil. The whole American Southwest had just been added to the Union. Would the Missouri Compromise hold? The abolitionists disliked it as an immoral bargain with evil. Slave owners claimed that it was an unconstitutional limit on their right to take their "property" wherever they pleased.

Davis was seldom a man for compromise. Forget the old Missouri Compromise, he urged. Allow slavery to go where it would and reach its natural limits. He proposed a bill that would do exactly that, even in the Pacific Northwest.

On July 12, 1848, Jefferson Davis rose in the Senate to give the most important speech of his life so far. It lasted for two hours. In a detailed, well-organized, and forceful style, he tried to defend not only slavery but its unlimited expansion. Today, people wishing to know what Jefferson Davis stood for have no better source than his own words in 1848. His argument went as follows:

1. Davis's defense of slavery went far, far back in time. Slavery was ordered and approved of by God, he said. (Davis could quote both the Old and the New Testaments on this point.)
2. Slave owners could hardly be blamed for forcing people of another race into bondage. Originally, some black Africans had forced other black Africans into slavery. These people were then sold as slaves to white traders.
3. Slave owners had had nothing to do with the transportation of slaves to the New World. The horrors of the crowded slave ships—the chains and hunger and filth and disease and death—all could be blamed on profit-hungry shipowners and captains from the North.
4. In their wisdom, the writers of the Constitution had recognized slaves as property. The Constitution also stated that a person could not be deprived of property "without due process of law." Thus, any citizen

61

had a right to take any property he wished into any territory owned by the United States.

5. Black slaves in the South enjoyed a higher standard of living than any other black people on the face of the earth. Free blacks in the North were forced to live lives of poverty, crime, and persecution.

6. Slavery could not be objected to on Christian grounds. Indeed, according to Davis, slavery had brought the black race from "the heathen darkness which hangs like a cloud over the country in the interior of Africa to the enjoyment of all the blessings of civilization and Christianity."

7. Northerners truly interested in the welfare of black people should welcome the extension of slavery. What would happen if slavery was limited to the states where it was already permitted? Davis argued that more and more slaves would then be owned by the same number of planters. Thus the close owner-slave relationship that Davis liked would be destroyed. An owner who did not know his slaves by name would be less concerned with their happiness and their comfort in old age.

8. Here and there, now and then, it was right for an educated and able black person to be granted freedom. But for most blacks, Davis stated, freedom "would be their greatest curse." It was the duty of the "superior race" to care for those less fortunate. It would be unfair to black people to expect them to compete with whites on an equal basis.

Davis ended his speech with the hope that Congress would act soon to end the differences between South and North. If this did not happen, the Southern states would have no choice but to leave the Union and form their own nation. Such a break should be a peaceful one, with understanding and friendship on both sides. Worst of all would be "the blood of civil war."

Thus, as early as 1848, Davis was warning the nation that war might be the final answer to its problem. Not that he wanted war.

A slave wedding held at the Davis plantation. Davis believed that whites were superior to African Americans.

Far from it. Most of all, he wanted the "constitutional liberties" of slave owners honored in the territories. If that failed to happen, he wanted a peaceful separation between North and South. Bloodshed would occur only if the Northern states refused to let the Southern states go their own way. Davis had drawn an "I dare you" line across the troubled face of a dividing nation.

63

CHAPTER SEVEN

The 1850s: From Compromise to Collapse

By 1850 two compromises had been reached. The first concerned the union between Varina and Jefferson Davis. The second concerned the Union itself.

The compromise with Varina seems to have been made largely on Jefferson's terms. True, by 1850 she was living in the new Brierfield—not as large a house as she might have liked, but not one she had to share with Amanda either. Her other demands, however, were forgotten or withdrawn. Varina wrote Jefferson in 1849 that she was reading a book called *A Guide to Social Happiness*. It would, she hoped, make her a better wife. Jeff was now "my sweetheart, my better life, my nobler self." She had been a "thoughtless, dependent wife" who "never knew the vastness of my treasure until now." By this time Varina had probably decided that any wife of Jefferson Davis would have to be exactly the kind of wife he wanted. From now on she would work tirelessly for his happiness, his health, and his career. When Davis returned for the 1849-50 Senate session, Varina traveled to Washington with him.

Absolutely nothing about the other compromise pleased Jefferson Davis. This was the famous Compromise of 1850, proposed by Senator Henry Clay of Kentucky. It was supposed to offer something to the South, something to the North, and be a way to live in peace for years. But Davis believed that it gave the South almost nothing. California was admitted to the Union as a free state. This, according to Davis, broke the old Missouri Compromise, because the southern part of California was south of latitude 36° 30' . Davis wanted California split into two states, with the southern portion allowing slavery. Also, the Compromise of 1850 permitted the rest of the land won in the Mexican War to be organized into territories with no mention of slavery. When those territories became states, they could decide whether or not to allow slavery. Davis thought this a bad idea; he wanted the "constitutional liberties" of slave owners written down in black and white. The Compromise of 1850 also included a new and stronger fugitive slave law, intended to please the South. Davis doubted that most Northern states would seriously enforce a law designed to send escaped slaves back to their Southern masters. Antislavery Northerners, such as Senator William H. Seward of New York, opposed any compromise with slavery.

Senator Davis argued against the Compromise of 1850 for months. He had a lot of support. From South Carolina and Georgia came calls for secession—leaving the Union—if the compromise passed. But in the end, Davis could not persuade enough senators to vote his way. He could not even count on the support of an old Southern friend, Zachary Taylor, who now sat in the White House as the last Whig president. Most certainly, he could not persuade the other senator from Mississippi, Henry S. Foote. Davis had always thought Foote a rascal of the worst order—a man who believed in nothing except his right to tell the right lie to the right voter at the right time.

Since their fistfight in 1847, relations between Davis and Foote had grown steadily worse. Now Foote favored the Compromise of 1850. On the Senate floor, the two men argued about who really spoke for the people of Mississippi. The battle went on outside the Senate. After breakfast one morning, another exchange of insults nearly became a fight. Davis swung at his short, stout enemy with his crutch. Foote's wig went sailing across the room. Friends separated the two men with nothing worse than shouted insults.

When Congress finally passed the measures that made up the Compromise of 1850, Foote saw a wonderful political opportunity. Across the country, compromise was quickly becoming the spirit of the land. Many people who had once disliked the Compromise of 1850 now agreed to accept it as the road to peace in the future. This was true even in the South. After all, if an antislavery senator like Daniel Webster of Massachusetts had extended the hand of compromise and friendship, why not accept it and get on with the nation's business? In Mississippi, Senator Foote and others in 1851 organized a Union Democratic party. This new party was made up of peace-minded Democrats and what was left of the weakened Whigs. Foote easily got the party's nomination for governor. He was a powerful speaker with a proven ability to get the needed votes.

Davis decided that Foote must be stopped at all costs. He spent most of the summer campaigning for the regular Democratic candidate for governor, a man whose chances against Foote were slim indeed. Two months before the election, the Democratic candidate, foreseeing certain defeat, dropped out of the race. Party leaders appealed to Jefferson Davis. To run for governor, Davis would have to give up his seat in the Senate. But he was their last and only hope against Henry S. Foote.

Davis accepted—even though at the time he was with Varina at Brierfield, dangerously ill. His swollen eyes could not stand light. He could not see to read. He spent his days in a darkened room and walked the floor by night. The old neuralgia knotted his face with pain. On doctor's orders, Varina nursed him with chloroform for the eyes, as well as five grains of quinine and two grains of opium a day.

Three weeks before the election Davis was still at Brierfield. By this time Foote's people were starting rumors that Davis was dead. Davis had to prove them wrong. Looking thin and frail, with a bandaged left eye and wearing thick green goggles, he rose to the challenge. Choosing his spots carefully, he toured the state and gave speech after speech. The Hero of Buena Vista was still a big name in Mississippi. By the November election, he had almost caught up with Foote—but not quite. He lost the state-wide election by a tiny margin, 999 votes in a total of 57,717.

Now Jefferson told Varina that he was tired of politics. He even hated politics. In the future he would stay at home and be the master of Brierfield, where he felt loved and needed. The faithful James Pemberton had died of pneumonia the year before, and the plantation had suffered from his loss.

Davis had promised to stay at Brierfield before, but each time he had been "called" to political office. The same thing would happen again, but this stay at Brierfield was to be a long one. It lasted well over a year. During the period, after seven years of marriage, Varina finally gave birth to a child. Little Samuel Emory Davis made her happier than she had ever been. Varina was a loving mother. And although Jefferson had always liked children, no one had expected to see such a proud glint in his healing eyes. It was as if he intended to make up to baby Samuel for the hugs and kisses his own father Samuel had denied him as a child.

The call to office finally came in late 1852. Davis's old friend, Franklin Pierce of New Hampshire, had just been elected President. Their careers had been somewhat the same. Both had served in the House, the Mexican War, and then the Senate. Now Pierce wanted Davis to come to Washington to talk about selec-

Franklin Pierce was President of the United States from 1853 to 1857. He asked Jefferson Davis to serve in his cabinet.

tions for his cabinet. Reading Pierce's letter between the lines, Davis was pretty sure he was being offered a job as secretary of war. Varina felt the old terror of having to leave home again. She loved the roses and pond lilies and white hyacinths of Brierfield. She loved their new house. She loved their daily horseback rides—and now Jefferson seldom beat her in a race by more than thirty seconds.

Davis said no to Pierce, but his old friend would not take no for an answer. More letters from Pierce followed, then telegrams. Varina held her breath, hoping against hope. Pierce finally appealed to Davis to at least be on hand for his inauguration in March. This request Davis could not deny. The Pierces had just lost a young son, their only surviving child, in a railroad accident. Davis, who had recently become a father himself, could understand what it would be like to lose a child.

When Jefferson Davis left for Washington, he may have thought that he wouldn't return to Brierfield for four years. At least Varina Davis thought so. She started closing up the house, to be ready to go when he sent for her. By now she was wise to the ways of Washington. She knew what was expected of a leading cabinet member's wife. There would be a huge rented house. There would be dinners and teas and receptions and parties for distinguished foreigners. It was hardly what she wanted, but she wanted most of all to be at Jeff's side. When her own call came, she bundled up baby Samuel and left for a new life.

Both friends and foes agreed that Jefferson Davis was an excellent secretary of war. Davis was a politician, of course, but he was also a West Point graduate with military experience. He persuaded Congress to increase the size of the army by half, to 15,562 men. He raised soldiers' pay. He worked closely with the commander of West Point, Colonel Robert E. Lee. He tightened controls on spending and supplies; it was soon said that no one could cheat the army out of even a brass button. He sent officers to Europe to learn the latest in weapons and warfare. He even imported camels for use in Texas and the Southwest.

Varina's success as a cabinet wife was just as complete. Jane Pierce, the president's wife, was frail and shy. Her nature and the recent loss of a third child left her ill equipped to lead

Jefferson Davis, the Hero of Buena Vista, served as U.S. secretary of war from 1853 to 1857.

Washington society. Varina quickly became a best friend. Jane Pierce loved little Sam, and they spent many afternoons together in the presidential carriage. Varina, Jane, and Sam would ride along the Potomac River or go to check progress on the Capitol Building. (Davis was in charge of adding the present wings and dome to the ever-growing Capitol.)

Varina also took on many of Jane Pierce's duties as a hostess. The twenty-two-room Davis house on Fourteenth Street was the scene of dinner after dinner. She entertained cabinet members, diplomats, and army officers. She tried to invite every member of both the Senate and the House to a reception at least once a year. She more than Jefferson liked the endless social whirl of

Washington. Her good looks and quick mind made her a hit at costume balls and other events. She not only made up for her rather stiff and formal husband but had real fun doing it. At a time when most women tended to overdo the ruffles, lace, bows, and frills, Varina liked to wear simple white. It set off her deep brown eyes and the red rose in her black hair.

Of course, there were disappointments as well. The worst blow for the Davises was the death of two-year-old Sam in 1854. The disease was a mystery; doctors could do nothing. Davis's crutches were long gone by now, but there were no crutches for this kind of wound. "For many months afterward," Varina wrote later, her husband "walked half the night, and worked fiercely all day. A child's cry in the street well-nigh drove him mad." But fortunately, Varina was already pregnant when little Sam died. In February 1855 a daughter, Margaret Howell Davis, was born. Friends again said that Varina was never so happy as when she had a new baby in her arms.

Serving in the cabinet instead of Congress meant that Davis did not have months of the year to spend at Brierfield. Instead, the Davises took vacations in the Maryland hills or in New Hampshire, often with Franklin and Jane Pierce. The two families developed a close friendship. Years later, Pierce would say that he always remembered little Margaret as the girl who bit the dog. Neither Varina nor Jefferson was in the room when the Davises' dog suddenly snapped at the toddler. President Pierce watched as Margaret got over her surprise, then went over and lay down beside the dog. Margaret waited patiently until she was sure the dog had fallen asleep. Then, very much on purpose, she bit the dog's nose hard.

Varina became used to walking in and out of the White House to see Jane, often every day. For different reasons, President Pierce often visited the Davis house, usually early in the morning or after supper. He wanted to seek Davis's advice on some important matter. One visit, however, was entirely different. In January 1857, Varina gave birth to another child, Jefferson Davis, Jr. Along with the baby came the snowstorm of the century. Friends worried about Varina's condition, but the snow was too deep to visit. Even Franklin Pierce couldn't keep Varina off his mind. Walking alone, the president left the White House and made his way through four-foot drifts. It took him an hour to walk a block and a half. When he finally got to the Davis house, he was relieved to find that Varina's condition was not much worse than his own.

Another person who helped Varina at the time was Senator William H. Seward of New York. Seward was a member of the new Republican party. Politically, the Senate floor had hardly been large enough to hold both him and Jefferson Davis. During the debate on the Compromise of 1850 it had been the antislavery Seward who so angered Davis by talking of a "higher law than the Constitution." Yet in a way, the two men admired each other. During the snowy January of 1857, Seward also worried about Varina. He saw to it that his own team of fine horses broke through the drifts in order to bring a nurse to Varina's side.

Less than two months later, in March 1857, Franklin Pierce's term as president was over. This meant that Jefferson Davis was out as secretary of war. But back in Mississippi, the state legislature had already chosen him as a U.S. senator. Davis simply left the War Office one day and reported to the Senate the next. Now he was no longer running a government department but back in the center of the ongoing slavery debate. And since his departure from the Senate in 1851, a lot had happened.

In 1852 a New Englander named Harriet Beecher Stowe had published an antislavery novel called *Uncle Tom's Cabin*. The book was a huge success. Millions read it. Many Southerners blasted the novel as a pack of lies written by a woman who hardly knew the South at all. In truth, probably, the book was no more true or false than Jefferson Davis's picture of slavery at Brierfield. Slavery differed a great deal from one place to another. Davis saw smiles on the faces of some slaves; Stowe saw welts on the backs of others. What matters historically is the enormous effect of *Uncle Tom's Cabin* on Northern minds.

There was a growing dispute over the area stretching from what is now northern Oklahoma all the way to the Canadian border. Action in the territories nearing statehood had centered on Kansas. It was a sad story. In 1854 Congress had passed the Kansas-Nebraska Act, the brainchild of Democratic Senator Stephen A. Douglas of Illinois. If Congress couldn't decide the

71

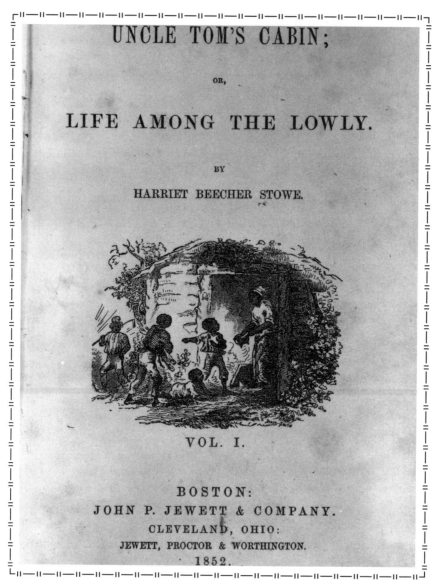

Harriet Beecher Stowe's antislavery novel, *Uncle Tom's Cabin,*
quickly became a best-seller around the world.

slavery question, Douglas reasoned, it should be left up to the
people in the territories themselves. He called his idea "popular
sovereignty." What could be more democratic? Let the people of a
developing state decide whether that state should be slave or free.

On the surface the idea had looked like a good one. But in fact, it led to disaster. Slave interests in the South and abolitionists in the North rushed settlers to Kansas. The territory soon became a kind of battlefield. In 1856 Southerners attacked and overran the "free" town of Lawrence. To get even, a Kansas abolitionist group headed by John Brown murdered five Southerners in cold blood. This angered Southerners, and the anger increased when Brown was never tried, or even arrested, for his crimes. The territory became known as "Bleeding Kansas." Two governments were formed, one slave and one free. Both applied for statehood.

About the time Jefferson Davis went back to the Senate in 1857, the Supreme Court entered the picture. If neither Congress nor the individual territories could decide the slavery question, maybe the courts could. Dred Scott, a slave held in Missouri, had spent some time in the free state of Illinois and in Wisconsin Territory (in what is now Minnesota) where slavery was not allowed. Returned to the slave state of Missouri, Scott sued for his freedom, on the basis that living on free soil had made him a free man. But the Supreme Court thought otherwise—no surprise, perhaps, because Chief Justice Roger B. Taney was a Southerner. The Court ruled that as a black person Scott could never be called a citizen of the United States and therefore had no right to sue. Moreover, he had never legally been a free man. He was property, and according to the Constitution, property could not be taken without "due process of law." Thus, neither Congress nor a territory could prohibit the spread of slavery. All past laws to prevent the expansion of slavery—including the Missouri Compromise—were ruled unconstitutional.

The South was overjoyed. The Dred Scott decision was just what slave owners had wanted for years. But many in the North were not about to let the spread of slavery be decided by a Southern judge and his Court. The new Republican party stood firmly against any expansion of slavery in the United States. Republicans like William H. Seward of New York and Abraham Lincoln of Illinois rode a rising wave of protest against the Dred Scott decision.

Back in the Senate in 1857, Jefferson Davis again took his place in the battlefield of words. The new President, James

Buchanan, was much like Pierce. That is, he was a Northern Democrat who often sympathized with the South, to hold party and country together. But the Democratic party itself was starting to split. Douglas of Illinois and Davis of Mississippi were more and more on opposite sides.

The strain of daily debate finally took its toll on Jefferson Davis. His voice gave out—completely. In early 1858 he took to his bed. Unable to speak, for a time he had to express his wishes by writing on a small slate. The painful neuralgia and the old eye trouble were worse than ever. He spent seven weeks in a darkened room, often in too much pain to eat. At one point Varina was sure his swollen left eye would certainly burst. (Doctors who attended Davis could do little, but today's doctors say his eye disease was almost certainly a form of virus. In simple terms, the virus attacks the eye and causes ulcers.)

Friends called often. Among them was Davis's old political foe, Republican William H. Seward of New York. Seward often came daily, to keep Davis up to date on Senate debates. Varina, too, was fond of Seward. One day, in her teasing way, she asked him if he really believed all he said about slavery on the Senate floor. Of course not, Seward replied, but that way of talking was the way to get votes from "the rank and file of the North."

Jefferson Davis struggled to raise his head from the pillow. "But," he said, finding his voice, "do you never speak from conviction alone?"

"Never."

"As God is my judge," stated Davis, "I never spoke from any other motive."

"I know you do not," said Seward sincerely. His gentle hands put Davis's head back to rest. The two friends understood each other well.

Recovery came with the spring, and summer brought a chance to escape the cares and heat of Washington. In early July 1858, the Davis family boarded a boat for Boston, then another for Portland, Maine. The fresh sea breezes worked wonders on Jefferson Davis's painful neuralgia and eye problems. The high point of the three-month trip was just that. The Davises spent some days living in tents on the top of Mount Humpback, in

Maine, where a good friend, the scientist Alexander Bache, was studying the stars. The cool, clear, absolutely soundless nights on the Maine mountaintop made Washington seem like a distant and dismal dream. Davis was thoroughly happy. A little sight even returned to the bad left eye.

Davis felt well enough now to resume speaking. He gave a talk in Portland and was amazed at the friendliness of the Maine people. On the return trip, he was asked to speak at Boston's famed Faneuil Hall. There, where many an abolitionist had brought cheering crowds to their feet, he presented his long, long defense of slavery. He also spoke at length of the shared history and many ties between New Englanders and the people of the South. His plea for peace in the future brought loud applause. Many Bostonians might not have liked all of the message, but they did admire the man. The same thing happened a few days later in New York City.

The next year, 1859, brought some good news— and much more bad. The good news was that, in April, Varina gave birth once again, in Washington, D.C. Her husband insisted on giving the name: Joseph Evan Davis. When the baby was born, Jefferson had been called back to Brierfield, to help fight the worst flood in Davis Bend history. Cattle, equipment, furniture, slaves—all had to be moved. Varina wrote that the baby was fine, but the name Joseph was not. For years she had disliked Jeff's older brother. Now she wrote teasingly that the poor baby even looked like Joseph. Too much unruly black hair. Too big a nose. In short, ugly. She hoped he would not take after Joseph in other ways: "I pray he may grow out of the resemblance." But the name of her son stayed the same.

The United States of America did not. In October 1859, John Brown raided Harpers Ferry.

John Brown was the bearded, stone-faced abolitionist who had shot five non-slave-owning but proslavery Southerners on the Kansas prairie. By October 16, 1859, he had formed an "army" of about two dozen whites and blacks. During the night he attacked the U.S. Army arsenal at Harpers Ferry, Virginia. (That part of Virginia is now West Virginia.) His hope was that nearby slaves would come running to the arsenal, seize the weapons

75

stored there, and form a real army in the Virginia mountains. From there, a slave revolt would spread throughout the South.

Nothing like that happened. Brown easily seized the arsenal. He even seized local people, white and black. But no slaves came running to take up his cause. Instead, the U.S. military came to blast Brown and his men, who were barricaded in a brick railroad building. Colonel Robert E. Lee soon forced a surrender. Only four of Brown's men were alive and uninjured. Brown himself was quickly tried and hanged for treason.

John Brown—without the long beard that was his trademark— shows his steely determination in this early photo.

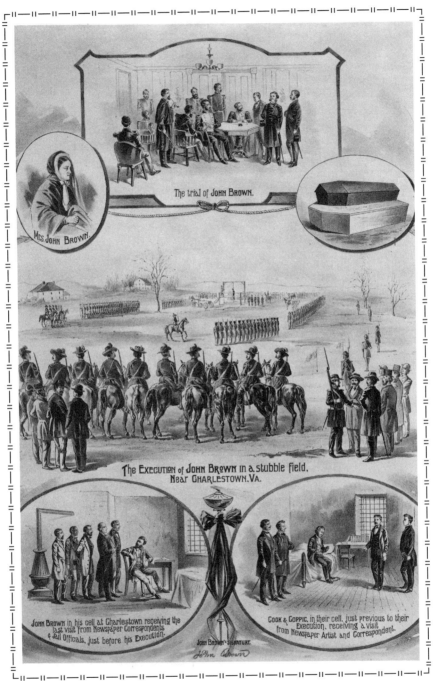

John Brown's raid on Harpers Ferry and his trial convinced some that he was a fanatic; others considered him a hero.

77

By December 2, the day the noose ended life in John Brown's body, the entire country lay in shock. In the North, abolitionists were calling John Brown a saint. But in most of the South, Brown was considered a madman. He was called the tool of Northern abolitionists who now wanted war.

Jefferson Davis served on a Senate committee to look into John Brown's raid. Some Southerners wanted to prove that Brown was an agent of an abolitionist group or even of the Republican party. According to the Senate committee, however, facts proved that Brown and his "army" had acted alone. Some well-meaning Northerners had given Brown money, but they had had no idea of his plans.

In Washington that winter, the dances and the parties nearly stopped. A chill had spread over the nation. With spring came increasing suspense. Everything now depended on the presidential election in November. The Republican's choice, most people thought, would be William H. Seward. He would get votes only in the North. Wanting to hold the country together, Davis saw another Democrat like Pierce or Buchanan as their only hope. If Democrats North and South could agree on a candidate, they could win the election.

But this was not to happen. The Democrats gathered in Charleston, South Carolina, in April 1860. Southern Democrats refused to accept the "popular sovereignty" of Senator Stephen A. Douglas. Northern Democrats refused to accept the Supreme Court's Dred Scott decision as the law of the land. As a result, the Charleston convention broke up without selecting a candidate. In June, the Northern and Southern Democrats met separately. The Northerners chose Douglas, as expected. The Southerners nominated John C. Breckinridge of Kentucky, who had been Buchanan's vice-president.

Making things still more complicated, a new Constitutional Union party met by itself and nominated John Bell of Tennessee. Its supporters condemned those who favored only their own section of the country.

Meanwhile, the Republicans had met in Chicago and nominated Abraham Lincoln, Illinois's favorite son. Lincoln was a new name to many in the South. Southerners feared that those opposing the Republicans would split their votes, resulting in a victory for Lincoln. Jefferson Davis made a last-minute effort to unite the opposition to Lincoln. He asked Breckinridge, Bell, and Douglas to give up their own hopes and come together to support a single anti-Lincoln candidate. The first two agreed, but Douglas did not.

In the November election, Lincoln carried the entire North, but he got not a single electoral vote in ten Southern states. Although he won only 40 percent of the popular vote, the electoral college gave him a commanding 180 votes—to 72 for Breckinridge, 39 for Bell, and only 12 for Douglas. Thus, as far as the popular vote went, Lincoln was not a clear winner; he just had more electoral college votes than any of the others.

Lincoln's earlier statements now brought panic to Southern ears. " 'A house divided against itself cannot stand.' I believe this government cannot endure permanently half slave and half free." The South was quick to prove him right. South Carolina was out of the Union by December 2. Mississippi, Florida, Alabama, Georgia, Louisiana, and Texas followed in short order.

Many Southerners greeted the South's separation with cries of joy, brass bands, and fireworks. Not Jefferson Davis. He loved the nation and his dream of what it should become. His father had fought for the new nation in the Revolutionary War. Three of his brothers had defended the flag in the War of 1812. He himself had won fame in the Mexican War. He had many good friends in the North. When the official announcement of Mississippi's secession reached him, he was again in bed in a darkened room. Against his doctor's orders, he dressed and went to the Senate for the last time. Years of argument had come to a sad end. Davis thought that secession was now the only path for the South to take, but it was hardly a happy one. Davis had no choice but to resign from the Senate. His final, short speech was a plea for peace, an expression of regret and friendship. It was greeted with applause from many, tears from more than a few.

The next morning Jefferson and Varina Davis boarded a train headed southwest. Once again, they went back to Brierfield.

CHAPTER EIGHT

The Rise . . .

Daffodils and early camellias were blooming on the Brierfield grounds that February afternoon in 1861. Working together on some rosebushes, the owner and his wife looked like the picture of peace. The man was now fifty-two. His hair was more silver than brown. A neat gray beard hung from the very bottom of his chin. The hollow cheeks were finely wrinkled, very

Soon after Mississippi seceded, Jefferson Davis resigned from the U.S. Senate and returned to his home state.

pale, and a gray film veiled the left eye. The body was straight as a broomstick and nearly as thin. In this the man differed from the woman, who had become comfortably plump. She was thirty-four now, a mother by nature and choice, and once again she was pregnant.

They were taking cuttings to make the rosebushes of the future. And as they worked, the future must have been very much on their minds. For Varina, the children probably came first. The oldest, Maggie, was now nearly six. She was still the little devil of the family, but a likable one. Four-year-old Jeff was a happy, satisfied child, much easier than his sister. Little Joe, now almost two, seemed to have more sparkle and drive. The toddler of the family was already his father's favorite.

For Jefferson Davis also, the family always came first. At least that's what he kept saying. But Varina must have wondered. On their way to Brierfield, Jeff had stopped at Jackson, the capital of Mississippi. There he had been named a major general, head of the Army of Mississippi. Varina knew that what he really wanted was to be general-in-chief of all Confederate forces. Would he get the job? The news might come soon. Since February 4, representatives of the seceded states had been meeting in Montgomery, Alabama. The Montgomery convention was to write a constitution and then choose temporary officers for the new government.

Hoofbeats suddenly broke the silence. A messenger from Vicksburg pulled his tired horse to a stop and handed an envelope to Jefferson Davis. Varina watched him open it. He turned white, unable to speak. *A death in the family*, Varina thought. Then he started to talk, Varina said later, "as a man might speak of a sentence of death."

Jefferson Davis had been chosen to be President of the Confederate States of America!

He did not want the job. He had not asked for it—in fact, he had told people that he would be a poor choice. Varina knew his failings. He was too stiff, too formal for the wheeling and dealing of politics. His sense of being always right offended others. Outside of his family, he was a hard man to love.

But he was also a man of great experience and courage. Experience and courage were just what the South needed at the

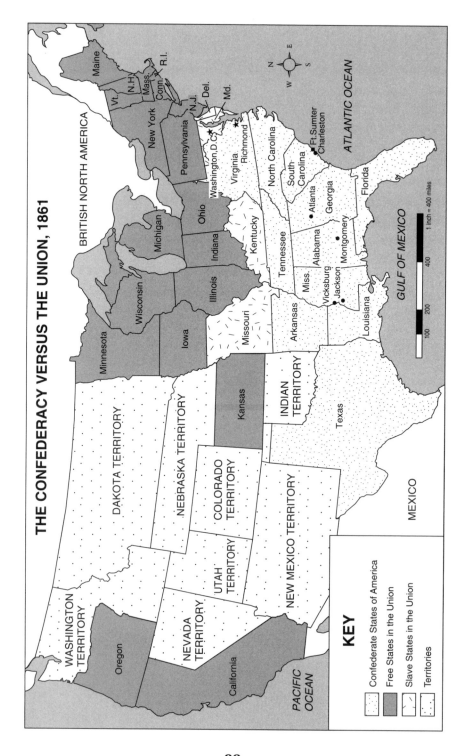

THE CONFEDERACY VERSUS THE UNION, 1861

KEY

Confederate States of America

Free States in the Union

Slave States in the Union

Territories

time. In fact, the Montgomery convention had seriously considered no one else. The others, after all, were politicians. Davis had always had a certain quality of lofty honor about him that separated him from other men in politics. This honor is what resulted in his being chosen on February 9, 1861, and what now made him take the job at once.

He left the next day. Varina and the children would follow. From Vicksburg there was a railroad east to Jackson. But there was no railroad to take Davis from Jackson two hundred miles farther east to Montgomery, Alabama. His train trip went east across Tennessee, down to Atlanta, Georgia, and then back west to Montgomery—seven hundred miles. Southern railroads had never been the nation's best. The system was a patchwork: short lines, different gauges of track, and awkward transfers between stations in cities where two lines didn't quite meet.

As he rode along, Davis must have thought with envy of the superior railroads of the North. If secession was to mean war, that would be a big advantage. In fact, on paper at least, the North seemed to have all the advantages. The advantage in railroads was three to one. The advantage in population—not counting slaves—was four to one. In manufacturing it was ten to one. From shoes to steam engines, from paper and pens to weapons and wagons—nearly all the products needed to fight a war were made in the North, not the South.

How, then, did Davis and other Southern leaders dare risk a war with the powerful North?

First, many Southerners thought it would be a war of words only. Would the North really send troops to kill other Americans? This was hard to imagine. Many Northerners agreed with Horace Greeley's powerful *New York Tribune*: "Wayward sisters, depart in peace!" Southern leader Leroy C. Walker was saying he would personally wipe up all the blood spilled as a result of secession with his pocket handkerchief.

Second, in spite of the North's advantages, the South was still strong enough to put up a good fight. Southern boys had grown up with horses and guns. Southern officers, from George Washington on, had usually been the army's heroes. The South would meet the Northern invaders with a hail of gunfire. The

North would lose many lives—sons, husbands, loved ones. How many lives would it take? Ten thousand? Fifty thousand? Sooner or later, the North would decide that peace was a better choice.

Third, the South believed that it had an unconquerable friend in old King Cotton. Without Southern cotton for Northern mills, many people would lose their jobs. The unemployed would scream for cotton and peace. The same thing would happen in England. Millions of British mill, textile, and clothing workers depended on Southern cotton for their jobs. They would force the British government to recognize the Confederacy and defend its rights.

Finally, Jefferson Davis and others believed that their cause was absolutely right. The word *right*, like the word *honor*, had always been something to fight for in the South. The U.S. Constitution had given certain limited powers to the national government, but "the powers not delegated to the United States by the Constitution, nor prohibited by it to the States, are reserved to the States respectively, or to the people." It followed that it was the right of a state to secede, since the Constitution said nothing about the matter. In fact, it was the North that had first broken the Constitution by meddling with slavery in the ter-ritories—about which the Constitution also said nothing. Jefferson Davis himself said that he now had to choose between the Union and the Constitution. He chose the Constitution.

"The man and the hour have met." So spoke William L. Yancey of Alabama when Davis reached Montgomery on February 18, 1861. "Prosperity, honor, and victory await his administration." Yancey, a secessionist for years, had himself hoped to be the Confederate president. But now he and others put on a great show of unity. Two days later came the formal inauguration of Davis as provisional president. Mounted soldiers led the big parade. Bands played. Thousands cheered. Women and girls threw flowers at Davis as he passed in a carriage pulled by six white horses. Behind him came the governors of the seced-ed states. A German-born bandmaster had just written a band arrangement of a little-known song. It turned out to be "Dixie."

The new government soon got down to business. Cabinet officers were appointed and started work. A Confederate flag was

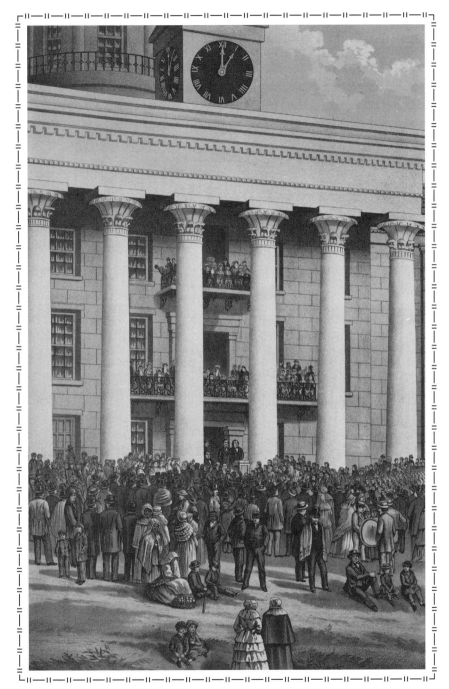

Jefferson Davis was inaugurated as provisional president of the
Confederate States of America in Montgomery, Alabama.

approved. Although the Alabama State House was the official national capitol, space there was limited. Davis's own office was on the second floor of a nearby market building. On the door was a handwritten sign on a plain piece of paper, "The President." Davis was a great man for details, and his days were long.

There was no immediate danger. President James Buchanan had done little about secession and would continue to do little. Weeks remained before Lincoln's inauguration. The Union army numbered only about 20,000 men with officers included. But about 3,000 of the 4,000 officers joined the Confederate forces, as did about 1,000 of the enlisted men. The Union army also had to keep some of its remaining troops on the western frontier. For a while travel was still possible between North and South. Southerners hurried North to buy guns and ammunition where they could. When Varina arrived in Montgomery, she ordered a $1,300 carriage from Newark, New Jersey.

War was still a possibility; it was not yet a certainty. When Lincoln became President on March 4, he addressed the South in the friendliest way he thought possible. He had no plans to interfere with slavery where it already existed. Yet he also had no plans to recognize a group of seceded states that called itself a separate country.

If war did come, Davis knew, it would have to start somewhere. Someone would have to fire the first shot. All over the South, Union troops had withdrawn from arsenals, army posts, and forts. However, the North still held Fort Sumter, an armed island in the harbor of Charleston, South Carolina. That state had been the first to threaten and the first to secede and might well be the first to fight. Davis offered to bargain with the North over Fort Sumter. He was even willing to pay for it. But Lincoln had no interest. How could the Union make a deal with a government it did not even recognize?

In early April, Davis learned that Lincoln was sending ships to resupply Fort Sumter. He quickly called a cabinet meeting. The decision was that the South now had no choice. The North's continuing occupation of a fort on Southern soil was itself an act of aggression. The supply fleet now invading Southern waters was another. President Jefferson Davis gave the order to his general at

Charleston, Pierre G. T. Beauregard: Give Sumter one last chance to surrender. Then fire.

Just before daybreak on April 12, 1861, the first shot of the Civil War was aimed at Fort Sumter. For the people of Charleston, it was like a Fourth of July rocket. In the dawn's early light the whole city turned out, dressed for a real celebration. From streets, docks, and rooftops, people cheered as the gray, smooth-sided rock far out in the harbor took hit after hit. Fire returned by Sumter was more of a bark than a well-aimed bite. It killed no one. The shore cannons boomed throughout the day, all night, and into the next day. In early afternoon the Union flag was blasted from its pole. Soon after appeared the white flag of surrender.

After the fall of Sumter events moved fast. On April 15, Lincoln

The bombardment of Fort Sumter in Charleston Harbor. Within thirty-three hours the U.S. fort surrendered

President Jefferson Davis's cabinet meets with Robert E. Lee, who resigned from the U.S. Army after Virginia seceded.

ordered a call for 75,000 troops to "put down the rebellion." This was too much for Virginia. That large state had so far held back from secession. But now Virginia wanted no part in an invasion of other Southern states. Virginia seceded on April 17, followed by Arkansas, Tennessee, and North Carolina.

Jefferson Davis now seldom left his work before midnight. With one hand, he appealed to the North for peace—"all we ask is to be left alone." With the other, he prepared for war. He ordered up a force of 100,000 volunteers. These men had to be fed, housed, supplied, trained, and then transported to a war zone. Generals and other officers had to be appointed to lead them.

In May 1861, the Confederate government voted to move itself to Richmond, Virginia. The Davis family soon moved into one of the finest houses in the city. The three-story mansion had

The Richmond, Virginia, mansion where President Davis's family lived was called the White House of the Confederacy.

huge rooms with high ceilings. At first Varina tried to hold receptions nearly every evening, but the cost and strain soon became too much. Also, her overworked husband, when he did appear, often looked tired and withdrawn. Jefferson Davis liked to spend his little free time with his children. Important visitors soon got used to a child on his lap or at his knee. The kids had the run of the house. Among the many decorations were the statues of three Greek goddesses on the ground floor. The little boys liked climbing up the "pretty ladies" to kiss them.

Richmond was only 100 miles from Washington, D.C. Davis got frequent reports on the growing Union army camped outside Washington. Sooner or later, he knew, it would start to march south toward Richmond. The Confederate line of defense was at Manassas Junction, an important railroad center about thirty miles from Washington. General Pierre G. T. Beauregard com-

89

Jefferson and Varina Davis greet guests at a reception held in their Richmond home.

manded a Confederate force of about 20,000 men there. General Joseph E. Johnston led another Confederate force of 11,000 troops about forty miles from Manassas Junction.

The huge Union army, 30,000 strong, began its move on July 18, 1861. Soon Davis learned that a Confederate line had formed at Bull Run, a creek just north of Manassas Junction. Then the battle started. Jefferson Davis wanted to get to the front but illness, then important business, kept him in Richmond. Finally, on the twenty-first, he got away. The train ride to Manassas was maddeningly slow. Then came the roar of cannons ahead, the sight of smoke. Just short of the town the engineer stopped the train. By now confused Confederate soldiers could be seen all around. They looked tired and beaten, their spirits gone.

Jefferson Davis had to go on. But no, the engineer said. What about the other passengers? Could he risk their lives? In desperation, Davis appealed to the others. He looked at an old man who somehow seemed courageous. The old man shook his head.

Then Davis asked the engineer if the train's engine could be separated from the cars. Of course it could. Davis ordered the engineer to do so. He and an aide hopped onto the locomotive to ride on toward the battle. They pushed ahead against a steady stream of retreating Confederates.

Nearing the battlefield, Davis got a horse and found General Joseph E. Johnston's headquarters. What was happening? Only then did he learn of a great victory for the South. General Johnston's troops had been able to join General Beauregard's forces. True, some of the thousands of Southern troops had been beaten back. But the rest had held the line and then advanced. In particular, General Thomas J. Jackson had held his position like a stone wall. Davis rode forward to see for himself. Wherever he went, troops recognized him and cheered. In the distance he could see the Union army in disorderly retreat toward Washington.

The Battle of Bull Run—or Manassas, as the South called it— has well been called "a battle of blunders." The troops on both sides were green. The generals lacked experience. But it was a great victory for the South because it helped undermine Northern confidence. The North was not to try another march on Richmond until the following year. Yet the Southern battle victory soon brought about controversy. Many Southerners complained that the Confederate forces should have followed up their victory by quickly attacking Washington. President Davis, General Beauregard, and General Johnston each argued that one of the others was to blame for not doing so.

The war in the West went badly for the South. During that

This photograph of President Jefferson Davis was taken by the famous photographer Mathew Brady.

winter a little-known general named Ulysses S. Grant outfoxed the Confederates to take Fort Donelson in Tennessee. The Southern forces retreated into Mississippi. Several Southern newspapers blamed Davis's leadership for the losses. Then, in April 1862, came the great Battle of Shiloh in western Tennessee. Grant was attacked by General Albert Sidney Johnston, the man Davis thought the best general in the Confederacy. The first day of the battle went to the South. But late in the afternoon, General Johnston was killed. During the night, Grant was joined by another Union army. When the South was finally forced to retreat, Grant's army was too exhausted to follow.

Shiloh was the first large battle of the Civil War. The North had 13,000 casualties (killed and seriously wounded), the South 11,000. Reports said that the next day a person could cross the battlefield just by jumping from corpse to corpse.

Another disaster in the West came toward the end of April. Davis had always considered New Orleans so safe that only a small force was stationed there. Fortifications on the Mississippi south of New Orleans were supposed to hold without fail. However, on April 24 Captain David G. Farragut's Union fleet blasted its way past the Confederate defenses. This was an important naval victory for the North. The South's largest and richest city was now in Union hands. Meanwhile, Union naval forces tightened a blockade of Southern coastal ports.

In 1862, Lincoln was not about to repeat the mistake of Bull Run. By May a massive Union army of 110,000 was waiting and ready. "In ten days I shall be in Richmond," boasted General George B. McClellan. (Jefferson Davis had recently been elected to a six-year term as the regular—not provisional—president of the Confederacy and inaugurated in Richmond on February 22, 1862.) Davis's worry about the nearby Union army was enough for him to send Varina and the children to safety. As she boarded a train for Raleigh, North Carolina, Varina again held a new baby in her arms. William Howell Davis had been born the previous October.

Confederate General Joseph E. Johnston retreated slowly as McClellan advanced. When the guns could be heard in Richmond, Davis could no longer sit at his desk. At the Battle of

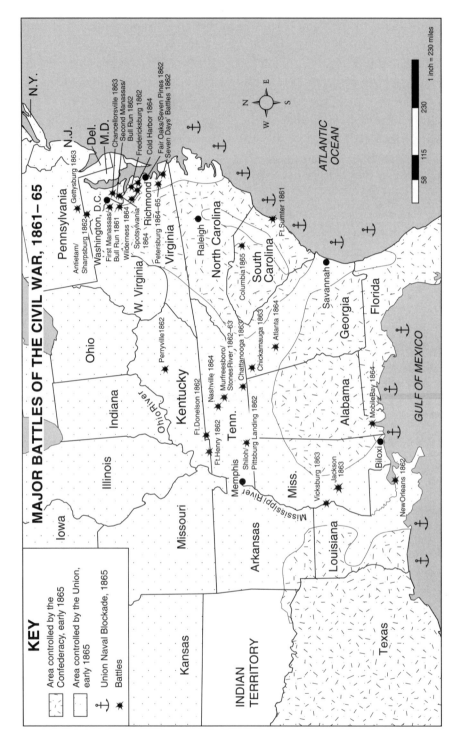

MAJOR BATTLES OF THE CIVIL WAR, 1861–65

KEY

- Area controlled by the Confederacy, early 1865
- Area controlled by the Union, early 1865
- ⚓ Union Naval Blockade, 1865
- ✳ Battles

1 inch = 230 miles

58 115 230

N.Y.

N.J.
Del.
M.D.

Gettysburg 1863
Chancellorsville 1863
Second Manassas/ Bull Run 1862
Fredericksburg 1862
Cold Harbor 1864
Fair Oaks/Seven Pines 1862
Seven Days' Battles 1862

Pennsylvania

Antietam/ Sharpsburg 1862
Washington, D.C.
First Manassas/ Bull Run 1861
Wilderness 1864
Spotsylvania 1864
Richmond
Petersburg 1864–65
Ft. Sumter 1861

W. Virginia
Virginia
Raleigh
North Carolina
South Carolina
Columbia 1865
Savannah

Ohio

Perryville 1862
Kentucky
Chattanooga 1863
Chickamauga 1863
Atlanta 1864
Georgia
Florida
MobileBay 1864

Indiana
Illinois
Ohio River
Ft. Donelson 1862
Nashville 1864
Murfreesboro/ StonesRiver, 1862–63
Tenn.
Ft. Henry 1862
Alabama
Biloxi

Iowa
Missouri
Memphis
Shiloh/ Pittsburg Landing 1862
Miss.
Mississippi River
Vicksburg 1863
Jackson 1863
NewOrleans 1862

ATLANTIC OCEAN
GULF OF MEXICO

Kansas
Arkansas
Louisiana
INDIAN TERRITORY
Texas

94

Fair Oaks (or Seven Pines) on May 31, he watched his soldiers check the Union advance. He also watched as General Johnston was carried from the field, badly wounded in the shoulder. The next day Davis replaced Johnston with General Robert E. Lee.

Lee's style of fighting was to move quickly, to outthink and then confuse the enemy. He was daring. He took chances. This was also the fighting style of "Stonewall" Jackson, with whom he soon combined forces. Lee and Jackson soon fell on McClellan in the Seven Days' Battles (June 25 to July 1, 1862). McClellan then retreated. Richmond was saved once again.

Generals Robert E. Lee (left) and Thomas "Stonewall" Jackson were two of the South's great Civil War generals.

Confederate hopes soared. By mid-August, Varina was back in Richmond. Later that month Lee again defeated a huge Union army on the old Manassas battleground. Thrilled by success, Lee wanted to press onward, to carry the war to Northern soil. He probably knew that his Confederate army was now outnumbered two to one. Its soldiers were ragged and often hungry. A fifth of them had no shoes. Yet Lee kept saying that with some reinforcements he could beat the Yankees on their own turf. Moreover, he hoped the people of Maryland, a slave state that had remained in the Union, would welcome and support Southern troops. Davis hoped so, too. He gave Lee the go-ahead.

So far, Lee had been unbeatable. A great victory on Northern soil might well end the war. Now Washington, not Richmond, would be threatened.

CHAPTER NINE

. . . and the Fall

That great victory was not to be. In mid-September 1862, McClellan caught Lee's army between the Potomac River and Antietam Creek. Lee had no room for his brilliant moves left and right. He had to stay in one place and slug it out. The Battle of Antietam (near Sharpsburg, Maryland) on September 17 was the bloodiest single day of the Civil War. About 23,000 people were killed or wounded. Lee was not defeated so much as he was stopped. The next day he began a retreat back into Virginia. McClellan did not follow up on this victory, and Lincoln removed him from command of an army.

Abraham Lincoln had been waiting for anything he could call a victory. He had an important announcement to make. Five days after the Battle of Antietam, President Lincoln issued his famous Emancipation Proclamation. As of January 1, 1863, all slaves in rebel territory were to be "forever free."

The Emancipation Proclamation enraged President Davis. Time after time, Lincoln had said that the war was not being fought to free the slaves. Now, Davis wondered, what was Lincoln doing? Davis thought that the proclamation was a cheap political move. The proclamation, Davis said, would result in the "extermination" of an "inferior race." Davis still believed that slavery offered black people the best life they could ever have in America. Free blacks would have to compete with white people. They could never succeed, he thought. Freedom would cause cruel suffering, even "extermination."

Lincoln no doubt believed that freeing the slaves would weaken the economy of the South. It would also boost Northern morale by giving Northerners a clear moral cause. The proclamation might also win the approval of important countries such as France and Great Britain, which might have sided with the South. Lincoln may also have thought that the Emancipation

President Abraham Lincoln issued the Emancipation Proclamation, freeing slaves in areas not under Union control by 1863.

Proclamation would lead to slave revolts in the South. If so, he was badly mistaken. Instead, the proclamation encouraged the Confederacy to fight even harder. And there was still a lot of fight left in the South. In December 1862, Lee and Jackson smashed a 113,000-man Union army at Fredericksburg, Virginia. The Union army marched south again the following April. At Chancellorsville, Virginia, a force of 130,000 collapsed before a Confederate army only half as large. Fredericksburg and Chancellorsville sent Southern spirits soaring. Winners should never quit, thought Robert E. Lee. Once again, Davis and Lee made plans to take the war to Northern soil. A big victory there would discourage the North and might well stop the war.

Gettysburg, Pennsylvania, was postcard pretty, a town of neat brick buildings. A small railroad ran to the east, and the town probably had shoes for some of Lee's 75,000 soldiers. Otherwise, Gettysburg had no military importance. It just happened to be the place where Lee's army met the troops of General George

Gordon Meade on July 1, 1863. During that day and the next the two armies scrambled for space. Neither side really won. Finally on July 3, Lee ordered a massive attack on a well-defended Union position. It was not a desperate move, rather a deliberate do-or-die choice.

The result was a disaster. Lee lost a third of his army, and he was lucky to escape with the rest. About 22,500 Confederate soldiers had been killed or wounded at Gettysburg. Never again would the South try for a victory on Northern soil.

The next day, July 4, there was more bad news for the South. Twenty-nine thousand Confederates had surrendered to Grant at Vicksburg, Mississippi. The North now controlled the entire Mississippi River. The Confederacy was cut into two pieces. The states to the west of the Mississippi—Louisiana, Arkansas, and Texas—would provide little further help.

The fall of Vicksburg brought a deeper sadness to Jefferson Davis. Vicksburg was the closest city to Davis Bend. It was where

Confederate troops suffered a crushing defeat at the Battle of Gettysburg in early July 1863.

99

he had started in politics. It was home. The year before, slaves had started leaving Brierfield when Davis's overseer panicked and fled. Southern troops had burned every bale of cotton to keep it from Union hands. Now, Joseph wrote, there were only six adult slaves left. There would be no cotton crop. Jefferson Davis would soon learn that the enemy had burned The Hurricane to the ground. Brierfield was left standing, but perhaps for a special reason. Union soldiers wrote THE HOUSE JEFF BUILT in big letters across the front of the building. It made a nice backdrop for those who could afford photographs to send home.

Other news was just as bad. It was clear by now that Great Britain would give the Confederacy no help at all. Davis had hoped that the need for cotton would force Great Britain to break the Northern blockade of Southern ports. But British cotton merchants, foreseeing the war, had purchased nearly two years' supply of cotton before the fighting started. Also, Davis had failed to understand the strength of antislavery feelings in Great Britain. That country had abolished slavery years before. Now Davis's diplomat came back to report that the British had not only read *Uncle Tom's Cabin*, but believed every word. Lincoln's Emancipation Proclamation had made ending slavery an important war aim; that also influenced British policymakers.

The home front, too, was falling apart. Here and there the countryside was terrorized by outlaw bands of soldiers who had deserted the army. All over the South, many women could not feed their families, even when their soldier husbands sent home every penny of their eleven dollars a month. The situation got worse as the paper money printed to finance the war went down in value. By the time of Gettysburg, the Confederate dollar was worth only eight cents. Sugar was twenty dollars a pound. In Richmond a chicken cost six dollars, a turkey forty. Flour went for three hundred dollars a barrel. There were shortages of everything. Women were making shoes out of corn husks and old rugs. The Confederate Post Office could not buy paper for stamps. In some cities there were food riots. In the countryside groups of penniless women often gathered their children together to fight for survival. Their letters brought home many a soldier who put feeding his family above winning the war.

The Confederate government printed more than one and a half
billion dollars in paper money to pay for the war.

After the capture of Vicksburg, Abraham Lincoln had brought
General Ulysses S. Grant east to take over the drive toward
Richmond. McClellan, a cautious general, had stopped before
totally defeating the Confederates after the Battle of Antietam in
1862. But in 1864 Grant refused to be stopped. Lincoln had
promised him an unending stream of fresh troops and supplies.
In May, Grant lost 17,000 men in a battle called the Wilderness
(near Chancellorsville) in Virginia. In this case, McClellan would
probably have called for a flag of truce. He had once written to
Lincoln that he tried to conduct the fighting "upon the highest
principles known to Christian civilization." Both sides would
have cared for the wounded and buried their dead. Instead,
Grant, with Lincoln behind him, thought that the way to finally

end the war was to press on and to stop fighting it one battle at a time. A few days after the Wilderness, Grant lost another 31,000 at Spotsylvania, Virginia. He kept pressing on. In early June, he lost 7,000 in a single charge at Cold Harbor, Virginia.

In a month Grant had lost 60,000 men. Lee, slowly retreating, had lost about half that number. Finally Lee dug in for a last stand in front of Petersburg, a railroad junction just south of Richmond. Grant lost 8,000 men in a mighty effort to break through the Petersburg defenses. He failed, but he did not retreat. There the two armies sat facing each other for another nine months. Lee's army grew weaker by the day as thousands deserted.

Jefferson Davis had now lost nearly everything but hope. He had lost the Mississippi River and the states beyond. He had lost most of Tennessee. He had lost most of Virginia north of Richmond. That spring he suffered a deep personal loss as well. Varina, as usual, was worried about his health. His old spells of illness had continued. At times he seemed torn apart by the war, unable to eat. Varina began to take a basket lunch up to his office on the second floor. For a few moments, at least, she could get his mind off the war and some food in his body.

Confederate fortifications captured by the Union army during the siege of Petersburg, Virginia, June 15, 1864.

Varina had just uncovered the lunch one day when the children's nurse came bursting into the room. Five-year-old Joe had fallen from a balcony to a brick terrace below. Both parents tore down the stairs and outside. Joe was still breathing, but the twenty-foot fall had badly crushed his head. He died in minutes.

"Not mine, O Lord, but thine." Davis repeated the words for hours, over and over and over. Little Joe had been his favorite child. That night he paced the floor till dawn. Unable to work, he then took a rare day off. Yet life had to go on—and it did. Jim Limber could wear Joe's clothing. Jim Limber was a free black orphan whom Varina had found—dirty, hungry, and scarred by repeated whippings—on the streets of Richmond. She had rescued him and taken him into the household to raise with her own children. Now there were only three of her own: Maggie, Jeff, and little Willie. Less than two months after Joe's death, Varina gave birth to her last child. Varina Anne, always called Winnie, was born on June 27, 1864.

Still, Jefferson Davis never lost hope. What was supposed to be a ninety-day war had now dragged on for three years. North and South, people were sick of war, disgusted with bloodshed. Davis's chief hope lay in the North. There would be a presidential election in November. The Democrats, opposing "Mr. Lincoln's war," were promising peace at any price. Their candidate was George B. McClellan, who had split with Lincoln and resigned from the army. Day by day the Northern peace movement was gaining strength. People wanted no more of General Grant's losses. Lincoln's own wife was calling Grant a butcher. In late August, Lincoln himself wrote that it was "exceedingly probable that this administration will not be re-elected."

Just days later, however, the tables turned. For months a Union army under William Tecumseh Sherman had been driving toward Atlanta, the capital of Georgia and a jewel among Southern cities. On September 2, Atlanta fell. Sherman's huge army moved on through Georgia—his famous march to the sea. The army took few losses and lived off the land. What was left of the eastern part of the Confederacy was cut in half.

People in the North now saw an end to the war at last. In his famous address to honor the men who had given their lives at

Gettysburg, Lincoln had said the war must go on to prove that "these dead shall not have died in vain." A year after that speech, on November 8, 1864, the Northern people re-elected Lincoln by 400,000 votes.

Still, Jefferson Davis felt sure the South could win. When the Confederate Congress sent a group of senators to Davis to urge surrender, he would hear none of it. Instead, he told the South that by the end of June the *Union* would be coming to him pleading for peace. There were still things he could do. Secretly, he sent a messenger to England with a new proposal. The South would free its slaves in exchange for British support. the British government had absolutely no interest. Another plan was to make Confederate soldiers out of black slaves. (The Union army was by this time nearly one-tenth black.) After the war, the discharged blacks would be free men. When the Confederate Congress finally approved this plan, it was too late.

Company E of the Fourth U.S. Colored Infantry. These Union soldiers helped defend Washington, D.C.

By March 1865, Lee had only 54,000 men at Petersburg, Virginia. Facing him, Grant had more than twice that number. The end was near. Members of the Confederate Congress lost hope and made their way homeward. Davis gave his wife a pistol and showed her how it worked. Then, on March 31, he put Varina and the children on a special train for Danville, a small Virginia city near the North Carolina line. With the family went young Burton Harrison, Davis's trusted aide. As they said their farewells, only Jefferson Davis could force back the tears. Little Jeff cried to be left with his father. Maggie clung to him as for her very life. Jefferson and Varina looked at each other for what they both thought would be the last time.

Two days later, April 2, was a Sunday. As usual, Davis attended St. Paul's Episcopal Church. As he sat waiting for the sermon to begin, a man walked down the aisle and touched him on the shoulder. Davis read the telegram handed him. It was from Robert E. Lee. Grant's army had broken through the Confederate defenses. Richmond would fall in less than a day.

Later that same Sunday another special train left Richmond for Danville. It carried what was left of the Confederate States of America: its president, some cabinet members, its treasury, and those files and records that could be quickly saved. A mounted troop accompanied the slow-moving train to Danville.

Meanwhile, Varina had moved on to Charlotte, North Carolina. By messenger she informed Jefferson that she and the children were safe and well. Her money would hold out for some time. If necessary, she would go ahead with their worst-case plan: Get to Florida and from there to some foreign country.

In Danville, Davis did his best to set up the government as though nothing had happened. He seemed calm, even cheerful at times. Where others saw the dark clouds, he saw the silver linings. Lee still had an army north of him. Joseph E. Johnston still had an army to the south. Giving up Richmond, Davis said, was actually an advantage. Lee would no longer have to defend the city. He could now fight Grant in his best quick-moving, hit-and-run style.

That wonderful silver lining vanished on April 9. Davis learned that Lee had surrendered at Appomattox Court House,

Richmond, Virginia. This photograph, taken in April 1865, shows the city soon after Confederate leaders had fled.

north of him in Virginia. Lee had really had no choice. His small, starving army was completely surrounded by an overpowering Union force.

Now Jefferson Davis himself really had no choice. Without Lee to defend Danville, it was a dangerous spot. What remained of the Confederate government moved on to Greensboro, North Carolina. This was the end of the line—the railroad line. Any trip farther south would have to be made by wagon, carriage, and horseback.

Generals Pierre G. T. Beauregard and Joseph E. Johnston came to Greensboro to discuss the military situation. Both saw no hope; they urged Davis to surrender on the best terms he could get. Four of the five remaining cabinet members said the same thing. But Davis still talked of combining what forces were left and then moving west. There was still a large Confederate army near Mobile, Alabama. With those troops to swell the ranks, Davis could move across the Mississippi River. There he would have an army of 100,000 men. The war could still go on.

Dreams! Dreams! Dreams! So thought the generals and cabinet members who listened to Davis talk. Now, in fact, even Greensboro was no longer safe. On April 15, the government left in a heavy rain for Charlotte. Most officials rode in carriages, but Davis insisted on a horse. He still had 3,000 soldiers with him, mostly cavalry. To the men riding at his side, he seemed at his very best—erect, alert, talkative. He talked about dogs he had owned. He discussed the fine points of horses. He told stories about the American Indian frontier and the Mexican War.

Arriving in Charlotte, Davis learned that Varina's party had left not long before. Then came really bad news: President Lincoln had been shot and killed in Washington. This saddened Davis, not so much for Lincoln as for the people of the South. He had believed that if the North won, Lincoln would treat the South "with malice toward none; with charity for all." He had his doubts about Lincoln's vice-president, Andrew Johnson.

Moving on ahead, Varina was not having an easy time. Varina and her children, with Jim Limber, a maid, and a nurse, were crowded into an old horse-drawn ambulance. Behind them came a wagon with their belongings. The countryside was full of Union patrols. Another danger came from outlaw bands of deserted soldiers. The old ambulance either bumped over stony roads or bogged down in the mud. Approaching Abbeville, Georgia, the mud was so bad that someone had to get out to lighten the load. The maid said absolutely no. The nurse was too sick. Varina herself got out. She wrote later that she "walked five miles in the darkness in mud over my shoe tops, with my cheerful little baby in my arms."

In Charlotte, Davis had what turned out to be his last cabinet meeting. He finally gave up the idea of resisting the enemy. Escape was now the only goal. He also wanted to find and protect his family. His 3,000 soldiers dwindled to ten men as he continued south, through South Carolina and into Georgia. His party was tracking Varina's, and he was slowly catching up.

On May 6, near Abbeville, Georgia, Davis learned that Varina was a short distance ahead. That was the good news. The bad news was a rumor that a lawless band of ex-soldiers planned to go after Varina's party that very night. Davis's small group rode on as fast as they could, the rest of the day and into a moonlit night. Long after midnight they saw some men in the road ahead. At first Davis thought they were the outlaws. Then one of them stepped forward. It was Burton Harrison, Davis's loyal aide.

The family reunion was hardly a joyful one. Every day they moved farther south. Davis wanted to stay with Varina and keep her safe. She wanted him to take off by himself. Alone and in disguise, he would attract far less attention. He would try to reach Texas. She would go to some foreign country, put the children in good schools, and then join him. On May 9 Davis agreed to Varina's plan. He intended to leave that very night, but his horse was too tired. The morning would be soon enough.

They stopped to make camp for the night near Irwinville, Georgia. Varina and Jefferson shared a tent, sleeping in their clothes for safety. With the first glow of dawn came the sound of rifle shots. Davis opened the tent and went out. Was it outlaws? No—Union cavalry! He stepped back inside the tent and reached for his raglan, a kind of sleeveless raincoat. In the dim light he got Varina's raglan by mistake. He put it on. Because the morning was cool, Varina threw her black shawl over his head. Then he walked

Northern cartoonists made fun of the Southern defeat. Davis was shown fleeing, disguised as a woman.

off at a normal pace, as if going to the nearby swamp for water. Thinking quickly, Varina sent her maid after him with a pail.

By now a few Union soldiers had come riding into the camp, poking around with interest. One of them, spotting Davis's handsome boots and sparkling spurs, rode toward him for a closer look. Davis threw off the raglan and shawl. The soldier drew his gun. Davis's mind worked fast: *Let him shoot. He'll probably miss. If he does, rush up, put my hand under his boot, and throw him off. Then ride his horse to safety.*

Varina stood looking at the scene: Her proud, strong-willed husband. A mounted Union soldier. And between them a gun—pointed in the wrong direction. She ran forward and threw her arms around Jefferson. He let her lead him back to the camp... and to whatever future there would be.

CHAPTER TEN

Man Without a Country

"We'll hang Jeff Davis from a sour apple tree."

Union troops had been singing the song for years. What actually did happen, for a man of Davis's pride, may have been far more painful.

Davis was taken by boat to Fortress Monroe on the Virginia coast. There he was placed in a damp whitewashed cell. Soon a Union captain appeared with four soldiers and a blacksmith. Davis saw at once that he was to be placed in leg irons. He threw himself at one of the soldiers in a struggle to seize his musket. It took all four guards to hold the prisoner down as the blacksmith worked with his shackles and chains. Then Davis sat on the edge of the bed, head in hands. "Oh, the shame, the shame," he kept repeating.

Fortress Monroe on the Virginia coast. There Jefferson Davis was imprisoned and, at first, kept in leg chains.

This nineteenth-century engraving shows Jefferson Davis arriving at Fortress Monroe by steamer from Savannah.

Years before, Davis had objected when the proud Sauk warrior Black Hawk was placed in irons. To him it was the final disgrace, in a way worse than death. In fact, he now wished he were dead. Guards paced back and forth outside the cell. An armed soldier stayed inside the cell at all times. A lamp was kept burning, even at night. Davis could communicate with no one, not even his beloved wife.

Meanwhile, Varina and the children were taken to a hotel in Savannah, Georgia. She was allowed little freedom. But unlike her husband, she could see the newspapers. These were daily doses of sudden shock. Jefferson was in chains. Because of the raglan and shawl, the story spread that he had tried to escape disguised as a woman. At the time of the capture, Union soldiers had broken open her trunks and suitcases. A hoopskirt had been found. Newspaper cartoonists put fact and fancy together to show Davis trying to flee in all sorts of outlandish skirts and dresses. Jim Limber had been taken from her, and now his scars were unfairly used to show how cruelly the Davises treated black people. A statement signed by President Andrew Johnson declared that Davis had masterminded the plot that resulted in Lincoln's death. Varina knew that this, like the rest of the rumors, was absolutely untrue.

Little by little, Davis's prison conditions improved. The leg irons came off. He had three comforts: his Bible, his pipe, and a kindly army doctor named John J. Craven. For weeks the physician was his only real company. Dr. Craven was amazed by Davis's great store of knowledge. From history and literature to plant life and birds—the prisoner seemed to know everything. John Craven soon became an admirer and good friend. It was through Craven that Davis communicated behind the scenes with Varina. When Davis grew very ill, the doctor insisted that he be moved from the damp cell to a comfortable room in a building on the Fortress Monroe grounds. Soon Davis was even allowed a daily walk in the sea-scented air.

When her restrictions were removed, Varina turned loose a torrent of energy. She sent the two older children to school in Canada; there they could better escape the long, dark shadow of Jefferson Davis. By letter and in person, she appealed on

Jefferson's behalf to the president, newspaper editors, and every politician she knew. After a year she was allowed to visit him at Fortress Monroe. Toward the end of his imprisonment, the government let the couple live together in one of the small apartments at the fort.

Jefferson Davis was indicted for treason by a grand jury in 1866, but he was never brought to trial. Finally, after 720 days in captivity, Davis was let go in 1867. There were good reasons for not bringing him to trial. First, in an effort to heal the nation's wounds, it was the Union's policy to go easy on Confederate leaders. High military and government officials had only to ask for a pardon and swear allegiance to the United States of America. If Davis were really guilty of treason, why weren't thousands of others? Second, a trial on the constitutional question of secession might have resulted in a verdict in Davis's favor. Finally, although many people disliked and even hated all that Jefferson Davis stood for, few thought that he was personally an evil man. Misguided and mistaken, perhaps, but far from a monster.

Dr. John J. Craven became Jefferson Davis's good friend during Davis's imprisonment at Fortress Monroe.

Davis spent the last twelve years of his life living at Beauvoir, a Gulf Coast mansion in Biloxi, Mississippi.

Davis could have returned to Brierfield for his remaining years, but he chose not to. The days of Southern planters living like millionaires on the labor of enslaved black people had ended for good. At Brierfield he would have been just another cotton farmer struggling to make ends meet in the ruined South. Instead, he went to Canada for a time, and then to England. Returning home, he tried this business and that, with little success. For a few years he headed a Memphis insurance company, but it, too, was not successful.

The last dozen years of Jefferson Davis's life may have been his happiest. He had always liked Mississippi's Gulf Coast. In 1876 Sarah Dorsey, an old friend of Varina's, offered to let the Davises live at Beauvoir, her shore estate near Biloxi. There Davis got down to work on the book he had wanted to write for years, a history of the Confederacy from his point of view. The work involved old papers, old friends, old memories that seemed increasingly bright. As the years passed, the book got longer and longer, until it was finally published in two large volumes. Unfortunately for Davis's fortunes, however, *The Rise and Fall of the Confederate Government* had a poor sale. Northerners didn't care; Southerners couldn't afford the stiff price. Also, much of the book was a tiresome rehash of Davis's old arguments. Secession was absolutely legal and far from rebellion. He even argued that slavery had had nothing to do with what he called the War for Southern Independence. The war had been fought to settle the conflict between two theories of constitutional government.

Right after the Civil War, a wave of dislike for Jefferson Davis spread across the South. Unable to blame the brave soldiers or generals like Lee, people pointed the finger at Davis. He had led them in a Lost Cause that many wanted to forget. By 1880, however, the wave was running the other way. In the 1880s, Davis was cheered by thousands as he spoke at the unveilings of statues

This family portrait shows (from left to right) Jefferson and Varina's married daughter Margaret and her son, Jefferson Davis himself, their daughter Winnie, and Varina Davis. A picture on the wall includes other children.

Jefferson Davis wrote a two-volume history of the Confederacy. Varina later wrote two volumes about her husband's life. Their daughter Winnie became the author of popular novels.

and monuments all over the South. He often appeared not with Varina but with the "Daughter of the Confederacy," his beautiful daughter Winnie. At Beauvoir, which was left to him on Sarah Dorsey's death, he received a steady stream of distinguished visitors. The frail old man still loved his horses and his dogs. Late in

Jefferson Davis lived to be eighty-one. His birthday is a legal holiday in several southern states.

the afternoon, he and Winnie could often be seen walking on the beach, throwing sticks into the waves for a couple of dogs that frolicked and barked.

In November 1889, Davis decided the time had come for another trip to see how things were going at Brierfield. Varina wanted to go along. No, Davis said, he might be eighty-one years old, but he felt fine. It would be just a short trip. He arrived at Brierfield with the chills and a bad case of bronchitis. After some days in bed, he was moved downriver to New Orleans, where Varina could care for him in the home of a good friend. Then pneumonia set in. Over the years Varina had nursed him through many an illness, but as the weeks passed she now grew discouraged. This time the stubborn old strength refused to snap back. In the evening of December 5, Varina gave him his prescribed medicine at the appointed hour. He swallowed a little but waved the rest away. "Pray excuse me," he said with his usual courtesy, "I cannot take it." Then he closed his eyes for the last time.

Right after their very first meeting, Varina had complained to her mother about Jefferson's "way of taking for granted that everybody agrees with him when he expresses an opinion." Davis remained opinionated and stubborn to the very end. He refused to swear allegiance to the United States. He refused to ask for a pardon; in his opinion, he had done nothing wrong. In his last speech, the spring before his death, he said it all: "I feel no regret that I stand before you a man without a country, for my ambition lies buried in the grave of the Confederacy."

Varina lived on for another seventeen years, until 1906. Now it was her turn to write two big volumes: *Jefferson Davis: A Memoir by His Wife*. She called herself Varina Jefferson Davis. To the disgust of some Southern friends, she spent most years after 1890 in New York City. There she turned out article after article for popular magazines. Proud, independent, interested and interesting —that was Varina to the very end. To her, people were people, not Northerners or Southerners. She bore no grudges. One of her best friends became Mrs. Ulysses S. Grant. And when she died, the funeral band played "Dixie."

1808	Jefferson Davis is born in rural Kentucky, the son of pioneer farmer Samuel Emory Davis and Jane Cook Davis.
1824	Davis enters the United States Military Academy at West Point, New York.
1828	As a young lieutenant in the U.S. Army, Davis begins a period of service on the frontier in the Upper Midwest.
1835	Davis resigns from the army and marries Sarah Knox Taylor, who dies three months after the marriage. His brother Joseph gives him land and help to start a plantation in Mississippi.
1845	Davis marries Varina Anne Howell of Natchez, Mississippi. He is elected to the U.S. House of Representatives.
1847	Volunteering for the Mexican War, Davis becomes nationally known as the Hero of Buena Vista.
1847-1851	Davis is chosen for the U.S. Senate late in 1847 and remains there until 1851.
1851	Davis loses election for Mississippi governor.
1853-1857	Davis serves a four-year term as secretary of war in the cabinet of Franklin Pierce.
1857-1860	Davis serves again in the U.S. Senate.
1861	Davis resigns from the U.S. Senate when Mississippi secedes from the Union.
1861	Davis is elected and inaugurated as the provisional president of the Confederate States of America.
1862	Davis is inaugurated as the regular president of the Confederate States of America.

1865-1867 With the fall of the Confederacy, Davis is imprisoned for two years at Fortress Monroe in Virginia.

1881 Davis publishes his huge history of the Confederate government.

1889 At the age of eighty-one, Jefferson Davis dies in New Orleans, Louisiana.

GLOSSARY

abolitionist   A social reformer who spoke out against slavery and worked to end it.

arsenal   An arms storage center.

court-martial   A military court called to try and punish offenses committed by members of the armed forces.

demerit   A mark placed on a person's record for some fault or wrongdoing.

dormer window   A window placed upright in a sloping roof.

electoral college   A group elected by the voters to do the actual selecting of the president and the vice-president of the United States.

emancipation   Freeing from slavery.

favorite son   A candidate supported by the delegates or voters of the candidate's own area of residence.

grand jury   A group of jurors whose task is to decide whether there is enough evidence for a trial. It does not decide whether a person is guilty or not.

indict   To present a grand jury's written accusation that the person named has committed a crime.

letter of resignation   A letter saying one is quitting a job.

mess   A group of people who regularly take their meals together, or the place where meals are regularly served to a group.

militia   Temporary citizen-soldiers called for service in emergencies, in contrast to regular troops.

planter   A person who owns a plantation, a large farm usually worked by laborers who live on the farm.

popular sovereignty   A pre–Civil War theory that people living in a newly organized territory have the right to decide by vote of their territorial legislature whether or not slavery should be permitted there.

secession   The withdrawing by a state from the Union.

states' rights   All rights not given by the Constitution of the United States to the federal government nor forbidden by the Constitution to the states.

tariff   A tax on imports (or a tax on exports).

BIBLIOGRAPHY

AND RECOMMENDED READINGS

Catton, Bruce. *The Civil War*. Boston: Houghton Mifflin, 1987.

Davis, Jefferson. *The Rise and Fall of the Confederate Government*. 2 vols. New York: D. Appleton, 1881.

Davis, Varina H. *Jefferson Davis: Ex-President of the Confederate States of America: A Memoir by His Wife*. 2 vols. New York: Belford, 1890.

Davis, William C. *Jefferson Davis: The Man and His Hour*. New York: HarperCollins Publishers, 1991.

Eaton, Clement. *Jefferson Davis*. New York: The Free Press, 1977.

*Green, Margaret. *President of the Confederacy: Jefferson Davis*. New York: Julian Messner, 1963.

*King, Perry Scott. *Jefferson Davis*. New York and Philadelphia: Chelsea House Publishers, 1990.

McPherson, James M. *Battle Cry of Freedom: The Civil War Era*. New York: Oxford University Press, 1988; Ballantine Books, 1989.

*Randall, Ruth Painter. *I Varina*. Boston: Little, Brown, 1962.

Ross, Ishbel. *First Lady of the South: The Life of Mrs. Jefferson Davis*. New York: Harper & Brothers Publishers, 1958.

Strode, Hudson. *Jefferson Davis: American Patriot: 1808-1861*. New York: Harcourt, Brace, 1955.

Strode, Hudson. *Jefferson Davis: Confederate President*. New York: Harcourt, Brace, 1959.

Strode, Hudson. *Jefferson Davis: Tragic Hero: 1864-1889*. New York: Harcourt, Brace & World, 1964.

*Tate, Allen. *Jefferson Davis*. New York: G. P. Putnam's Sons, 1969.

Thomas, Emory M. *The Confederate Nation: 1861-1865*. New York: Harper & Row, 1979.

*Especially recommended for younger readers.

Biloxi, Mississippi	• Beauvoir: The Jefferson Davis Shrine. This National Historic Landmark is the mansion where Jefferson Davis lived his last twelve years.
Fairfield, Kentucky	• Jefferson Davis Monument State Park marks the birthplace of Jefferson Davis. The monument is the tallest concrete-cast obelisk in the world.
Irwin, Georgia	• Jefferson Davis Memorial Park has a museum and a monument marking the site of Jefferson Davis's capture by Union troops.
New Orleans, Louisiana	• The Confederate Museum contains a memorial to Jefferson Davis.
Richmond, Virginia	• Museum and White House of the Confederacy. The mansion and adjoining museum contain furnishings and exhibits from the Confederate period, including an exhibit entitled "Victory in Defeat: Jefferson Davis and the Lost Cause."
Woodville, Mississippi	• Rosemont Plantation. The Davis family mansion contains furnishings and objects from the nineteenth century.

INDEX

Robert R. Potter, educator and author, has taught on levels from junior high through graduate school and has written eighteen books. He earned an Ed.D. from Teachers College, Columbia University, in 1965, and has held professorships at both the State University of New York and the University of Connecticut. For the past twenty-three years he has lived with his family in northwestern Connecticut. His hobbies include reading, model railroading, and the production of fine maple syrup.

James P. Shenton is Professor of History at Columbia University. He has taught American History since 1951. Among his publications are *Robert John Walker, a Politician from Jackson to Lincoln*; *An Historian's History of the United States*; and *The Melting Pot.* Professor Shenton is a consultant to the National Endowment for the Humanities and has received the Mark Van Doren and Society of Older Graduates' Great Teachers Award. He also serves as a consultant for CBS, NBC, and ABC educational programs.

COVER ILLUSTRATION
Gary McElhaney

MAPS
Go Media, Inc.

PHOTOGRAPHY CREDITS
p.6 The Bettmann Archive; p.9 State Historical Society of Missouri; p.11 Library of Congress; p.19 Mississippi Department of Archives & History; p.22 Courtesy West Point; p.30 Alabama Department of Archives & History; p.39 The Bettmann Archive; p.42 Mississippi Agricultural & Industrial Board; p.43 The Bettmann Archive; p.47 The Bettmann Archive; p.49 (Calhoun) Beinecke Rare Book & Manuscript Library, Yale University; p.49 (Clay) The Library of Congress; p.52 The Bettmann Archive; p.55 The Bettmann Archive; p.59 Wichita State University; p.60 The Library of Congress; p.63 Old Court House Museum Collection, Vicksburg, Mississippi; p.67 National Portrait Gallery; p.69 Brown Brothers; p.72 The Library of Congress; p.76 The Boston Athenaeum; p.77 The Library of Congress; p.85 The Library of Congress; p.87 The Library of Congress; p.88 The Library of Congress; p.89 The Bettmann Archive; p.90 The Bettmann Archive; p.92 The Bettmann Archive; p.95 The Library of Congress; p.98 The Library of Congress; p.99 The Library of Congress; p.101 (both) The Boston Athenaeum; p.102 The Library of Congress; p.104 The Library of Congress; p.106 The Library of Congress; p.108 The Boston Public Library; p.110 Fort Monroe Casemate Museum; p.111 Fort Monroe Casemate Museum; p.113 Fort Monroe Casemate Museum; p.114 The Bettmann Archive; p.115 The Bettmann Archive; p.116 The Bettmann Archive; p.117 Brown Brothers.